Doing Development in West Africa

DOING DEVELOPMENT IN WEST AFRICA

A Reader by and for Undergraduates

CHARLES PIOT, EDITOR

Duke University Press   Durham and London   2016

© 2016 Duke University Press
All rights reserved
Printed in the United States of America on acid-free paper ∞
Designed by Natalie F. Smith
Typeset in Quadraat Pro by Westchester Publishing Services

Library of Congress Cataloging-in-Publication Data
Names: Piot, Charles, editor.
Title: Doing development in West Africa : a reader by
and for undergraduates / Charles Piot, editor.
Description: Durham : Duke University Press, 2016. |
Includes bibliographical references and index.
Identifiers: LCCN 2016004516 |
ISBN 9780822361763 (hardcover : alk. paper) |
ISBN 9780822361923 (pbk. : alk. paper) |
ISBN 9780822374039 (e-book)
Subjects: LCSH: Economic development projects—Togo. |
Economic assistance, American—Togo. |
Duke University—Students—Travel—Togo. |
Togo—Rural conditions.
Classification: LCC HC1015.Z9 E443 2016 |
DDC 338.91096681—dc23
LC record available at http://lccn.loc.gov/2016004516

Cover art: School children in Farendé using the cyber café
built by Duke students. Photo by Sarah Zimmerman.

Contents

Acknowledgments

It will be hard to acknowledge everyone who has made this project possible because of its profoundly collective, organic nature. Almost forty Duke University students have gone to northern Togo over a period of eight years, each making small but significant contributions upon which subsequent generations built. This is truly an example of the sum being greater than the parts. A vast network of people in the villages made possible all that we achieved: the families who took the students in and treated them like royalty; the community partners and translators who attended assiduously to every need; those village youth who participated in the projects; local chiefs, and supporters in Lomé. Last but not least, this was all nurtured by a generous, well-endowed university that encourages and provides the opportunity for students to engage in small service projects abroad.

At Duke, we thank the units that funded the Togo projects: DukeEngage, Humanities Writ Large, the Global Health Institute, the Center for African and African American Research, the Center for International Studies, the Kenan Institute. Many thanks to Srinivas Aravamudan, Irina Adams, Sumi Ariely, Lee Baker, Lysa MacKeen, Elaine Madison, Randy Matory, Mike Merson, Eric Mlyn, Nancy Robbins, Kathy Sikes, Rob Sikorski, and Carrie Slaughter.

In Farendé, we thank the families: Marie Ali; Albertine, Rose, and Reine Katchawatou; and Justine Terao. In Kuwdé: Tikenawé Gnossi; Amélie Kansoukou; and Béa Welayaba (and their spouses and children).

The community partners: Cyril Hounlété, Jesper Karma, Elie Karma, Basil Pyake, Francois Kpamy, Kouwènam Basseliki, Georges Ebia.

The chiefs: Chef Canton Karabalo Batcho, Chef Village Kawabalo Nondahouleba, Chef Village Ntcharifei Koupe, Chef Quartier Kérékou Atakpai.

The DukeEngage site coordinators: Mackenzie Cramblit and Fidèle Ebia. Fidèle also coordinated orientations and homestays in Lomé from 2008 on. She is an incomparable resource, with superb judgment in all matters Togolese.

The special assistant: Pakétam Kourakoma. Pakétam has served as courier, chauffeur, mechanic, solar panel installer, tour guide, chaperone, scorpion and snake debugger, mollifier of soldiers—you name it. He is a prince in every way.

The students who spent summers in the north: Uzo Ayogu, Nathalie Berger, Connor Cotton, John Deans, Mona Dai, Michaela Domaratzky, Kalina Ehrenreich-Piot, Bradford Ellison, Geff Fauchet, Ebony Hargro, Tara Hopkins, Ruj Jiang, Anne Johnson, Isaac Keohane, Abi Lawrence, Charlotte Mabe, Madeline McCrary, Whitney McLeod, Mary Elizabeth McLaughlin, Allie Middleton, Caitlin Moyles, Evan Murray, Morghan Phillips, Ben Ramsey, Sean Rojet, Maria Romano, Stephanie Rotolo, Emma Smith, Alex Snider, Meggie Staffiera, Brian Tepera, Linda Zambrano, Sarah Zimmermann, and Carrie Wang. And those who were based in Lomé: Serra Aktan, Lizzeth Alcaron, Camille Anderson, Kelly Andrejko, Uche Anigbogu, Erin Boland, Petrina Craine, Aubrey Frazzitta, Nash Mepukori, Emmanuelle Noar, Houston Rhodes; and Anusha Singh; the family of Laure and Nicolas Batema; and the Apetoh, Petos, Tsolenyanu, and Zikpi families.

At Duke University Press, Ken Wissoker engaged this project at an early stage and made smart, encouraging suggestions for how to make it better. He also found reviewers who keyed into the unusual nature of the project— of students' essays dealing with applied topics—and who made astute, exceedingly helpful suggestions. There is no better editor in the land. Elizabeth Ault expertly shepherded the manuscript through the final stages of review and production.

Special thanks to John Hawkins, whose book of undergraduate essays on Guatemalan healing practices provided inspiration for our own; to Mark Noar, a Duke father, who has contributed enormously to the development of the villages, and whose efforts have complemented the projects described here; to Henri Bamaze, who seemingly knows everyone in Togo and is always there to run interference and offer sage advice; to Kalina, whose intuitive understanding of life in Kuwdé enables her to come up with smart insight and offer advice that is beyond her years. And last but not least, and as always, special thanks to Orin Starn and Anne Allison for their demanding critique and eternal support.

Introduction
Charles Piot

The number of U.S. university students traveling abroad for the summer to engage in small-scale development efforts in Africa, Asia, and Latin America has increased dramatically over the past decade. The students volunteer in rural health clinics; set up micro-lending initiatives; build schools and dig wells; organize the export of local textiles to markets of the global North—and the list goes on. Compelled by a mix of utopian and pragmatic desires, these students at once hope to help the world's poor while building résumés and finding adventure. A political movement by another name, perhaps.

This book—written by and for undergraduates captivated by the idea of do-it-yourself (DIY) development in the global South—describes projects undertaken by Duke University students since 2008 in two villages in northern Togo, West Africa. The projects are inexpensive and aim small, and they are tethered to a common theme: youth culture/youth flight. Among other efforts, these students have built a cyber café, organized a microfinance initiative for teens, set up a writers' collective, and installed a village health insurance system. They engage their projects with commitment and creativity—and with the courage it takes to live locally and subsist on food that is foreign to the palate, while also being exposed to tropical fevers and dysentery. They come from a variety of backgrounds (Anglo, Caribbean, Latin American, Asian, second-generation African,

African American) and a range of Duke majors (English, cultural anthropology, engineering, global health, physics, international comparative studies, African and African American studies), and there are invariably more women than men. They often do not know one another before setting out but typically develop deep friendships and work hard together to achieve their projects' aims.

Duke alone has ten or more group projects in Africa every summer, many sponsored by DukeEngage, a large civic engagement program begun in 2006 in the wake of the Duke lacrosse scandal.[1] The university also sponsors dozens of individual research and internship projects on the continent and has study abroad programs in Ghana and South Africa. Latin America and Asia have similar profiles. While there are specificities to Duke's programs, they share broad affinities and common desires with initiatives at other universities. Our hope in publishing these essays is that they will provide inspiration, and perhaps a model, for student development efforts elsewhere.

● ● ●

I never intended to be a development anthropologist. Brought up in the halls of high theory—Lévi-Strauss, Marx, Foucault, and Derrida were daily fare in my graduate school classes—I looked down on anything "applied," which not only seemed anti-Theory but also smacked of complicity. When I was first in the field in the mid-1980s, I ran the other way when I saw a development worker or a missionary. My generation of anthropologists was in search of alterity, of societies uncontaminated by capitalism (or by development workers and missionaries). We aimed to defend and give voice to other ways of being in the world rather than to change or colonize them. It was a noble cause, if also patronizing.

Now, many years later, I still like theory but I am also intrigued with missionaries and development workers—not merely as objects of study (although they are that, as well; I have written about development work in West Africa) but also as fellow travelers, for I have become something of a development agent myself. I have set up a fund in my fieldwork village, contributing royalties from book sales to a village development account, and I take students there each summer to engage in small development efforts. These students have installed an Internet café in one of the villages, set up a health insurance program in another, established a microfinance scheme, and organized a writers' club, among other projects.

So what changed?

Theory, for one thing. Today, anthropologists know better than to imagine that we might be able to access pure social forms outside entangled global histories—that there might be an uncontaminated outside to capitalism, that missionaries and development workers are not always already part of village landscapes everywhere. It is a foundational assumption of the discipline today that societies and cultures are always messy and mixed; that there are no outsides; and that entanglement and complicity are the norm.

Then, too, we have abandoned the naïve view that the anthropologist studying everyday life in a village might be a detached observer, having little effect on what he or she is studying. Today, we assume that the anthropologist herself is always implicated in the field of study, that she is constantly affecting those around her in a range of ways (through her data gathering, through the money and medicine she distributes, through discussions and conversations, through her social relationships). If researchers are already implicated, like missionaries and development workers, why would they not also want to take the next step and attempt to ameliorate the living conditions of those they care about?

But as significant for me are recent changes in student culture. Whether deriving from the cachet that the phrase "global university" has on college campuses today or from a desire to do good in the world, or both, today's college students are signing up for semester and summer abroad programs in record numbers. They work as interns, conduct small research projects, or attend study abroad classes, many in Africa and Latin America. At Duke, students flock to these continents each summer, thanks to two new powerhouse units on campus: the Global Health Institute and DukeEngage, a service-learning program that sends up to four hundred students a year overseas and has passed Duke Basketball as the number-one reason entering freshmen choose to matriculate at the university.[2] Projects like these are all the rage at universities around the country (Handler 2013), not just at Duke, and range from study abroad programs and health internships to volunteer work with nongovernmental organizations (NGOs). While there are specificities to each program, and to the locales where students end up, the programs are largely driven by common impulse: by students' desire to travel and learn and make a difference in the world.

It is easy to be cynical about this new student culture, this quiet social movement that aims to bring change through personal initiative. Is this enthusiasm not more about résumé building or adventure—"academic tourism," some have called it—than making a difference? Is it not driven by naive assumptions about development and what it means to "make an impact"? How can a U.S. college student, typically from the suburbs, parachute into a village in Africa or Latin America for a few months, with minimal local knowledge, and really hope to make a difference?

This is all true, of course, and I spend much of my undergraduate "Development and Africa" class criticizing the view that development can accomplish anything at all without a deep understanding of local culture, politics, and history. Yet I have also found the youthful idealism of the students I have been associated with irresistible and many of their projects inspiring. Moreover, whatever their motivations, their efforts are hailed by those in the villages where I conduct research, and their work has had a positive impact on local lives.

My involvement in student-led development started by chance—and because an administrator from Duke's Global Health Institute called my bluff. She showed up at my office one day to ask if I would mentor three of her students who were planning summer internships in Ghana, help them brainstorm their projects, and check in on them over the summer. I told her I was not keen on going to Ghana—getting there from Togo was time-consuming, and the roads were terrible—but that if she had students who spoke French and wanted to work in Togo, I would consider it. I assumed that was the last I would hear from her—that language would be a stumbling block—only to get an e-mail two weeks later saying she had six students interested in Togo, all with French-language skills. I agreed to speak with them, and won over by their earnest enthusiasm, I ended up taking three.

When they arrived that summer, I set them up with internships and homestay families, then left to do my own research, telling them I would return three weeks later to see how they were doing and to brainstorm a possible intervention. I wanted each to come up with a single idea she could work on during her last month that might make a difference in local lives. To my surprise, two of the students came up with quirky, brilliant ideas—a village health insurance scheme and a money-pooling system—that, in twenty-five years in the area, had never crossed my mind. One of these, the health insurance plan, was implemented the following year and is still in place today. Moreover, at the end of the summer, villagers pleaded with me to bring more students the next year. They were thankful not only for the projects but also for the money the students had injected into the local economy and for their good humor in the face of everyday challenges. Most important, they felt acknowledged by the fact that students from far away had chosen their village as a place of residence and work. "You've given us many small things over the years," a friend said as I was leaving for the start of classes that fall, "but bringing these students is the best thing you've ever done."

Inspired by the projects the two students had initiated and knowing they would need follow-up—but also sobered by my interlocutor's frank appraisal of my own long-standing attempts to reciprocate local generosity—I decided to bring another cohort the following summer. They turned out to be as good as the group before. And so it went: each year a new cohort brought new ideas and energy, and the projects kept morphing in interesting ways. Today, I have few regrets about this unexpected turn in career. Moreover, these students have opened new vistas for me—not only applied, but also theoretical.

A Brief History of Development in West Africa

If anthropology and student culture have changed since the 1980s, so has development. During the early independence period in West Africa (circa 1960–1990), economic development was top-down, state-driven, and large-scale, focused primarily on infrastructure such as roads, schools, and clinics. With the end of the Cold War and the drying up of state monies, however, development scaled down and went local—"to the grassroots," was the refrain—with NGOs replacing states as purveyors of development and development's focus shifting from infrastructure to education, health, and human rights; from things material to "immaterial." The end of the Cold War also brought a change in development's target population away from large groups such as nations, regions, ethnic groups or villages, all typically run by men, to women and youth, especially girls. Standard projects today in West Africa, many sponsored by European and American NGOs, target girls' education, the human immunodeficiency virus (HIV) and malaria, child trafficking, and microfinance.

Take, for instance, the villages in northern Togo where I have worked for many years—and where I have taken students. In the 1980s, the Togolese state was busy building schools and clinics, and its development agency, Affaires Sociales, had a salaried employee in every village. By the mid-1990s, the money had dried up and the state had withdrawn from the development field. In its place, a Danish NGO had opened a child sponsorship program (to send girls to school and provide their families with medical and food aid), and a German NGO had established a microfinance initiative to fund local entrepreneurs who lacked liquidity.[3] Notice, again, the shift from material to immaterial, from infrastructure to what the World Bank refers to as "human capital" (Benjamin 2007).

Contemporary economic development sits within a larger global political economy that scholars call "neoliberal" (Foucault 2010; Harvey 2007). Also referred to as the "Washington Consensus" by the World Bank and the International Monetary Fund, its main boosters since its inception in the 1980s, the neoliberal era is characterized by state pullback and decentralization, democratization, "NGO-ization," the privatization and marketization of almost everything, financialization and the emergence of the consumer citizen, and class consolidation and growing inequality (Harvey 2007). Across the global South, the neoliberal moment is typified not only by state withdrawal and the emergence of the NGO but also by a new "contract" between development and needy citizen or community. No-strings-attached charitable aid (the "free" handout) is a thing of the past, replaced by a quid pro quo—"We'll contribute materials, if you provide the labor," "We'll offer liquidity as long as you pay us interest," "Where's the proof that you have skin in the game?"—and needy citizens come to be seen as responsible for their own development. In Michel Foucault's (2010) felicitous phrase, the neoliberal subject is a "self-responsibilizing" one, the author of his or her own betterment.

A recent stream of development practice with relevance to my students' projects—and a distillation of neoliberalism's embrace of individual initiative, also consistent with the move away from the large scale and top down—is referred to as DIY development (Kristoff 2010). The DIYers are individuals, often recent college graduates with experience in the Peace Corps or working for an NGO, who decide to do it on their own, in the process circumventing the development apparatus. These self-starters identify a problem (lack of access to tampons in Congo, to bed nets in Benin, to the Internet in Togo);

set up a website, where they announce the project and raise money; and purchase and distribute the materials—all with little interference, thanks to the pullback of the state during the post–Cold War dispensation.

Again, there is much to criticize in this trend—in many ways, the apotheosis of development as we know it, the reduction of charitable aid to individual initiative—as it is dogged by all of the problems of development more generally. For better or worse, my students' projects are a version of DIY development, although I would like to think they are conceived and implemented with greater attention to local context and with a healthy respect for all that might go awry.

One of the widely acknowledged truths of development in Africa over the past fifty years is that it has failed, and dramatically so. Project after project after project has failed, more than 90 percent of them—latrines, energy-saving stoves, animal traction, poultry vaccination, irrigation initiatives, fertilizers, wells projects, labor cooperatives . . . The list goes on and on. More than $1 trillion has gone down the tubes, Dambisa Moyo (2010), the former World Bank economist, estimates.

There are many reasons for this calamity, including the long history of colonialism, an unforgiving environment, a global political economy that is stacked against its peripheries, government misappropriation of funds. But it is also due to the development apparatus's failure to appreciate—understand, take account of, spend time studying, articulate projects with—local realities. Euro-Americans love to imagine that technology solves all problems and that the solution to development's travails is technological. Introduce a cattle-pulled plow and farmers will rush to partake in its wonders; make fertilizer available and crop yields will increase; build energy-saving stoves and women will immediately sign on; make liquidity available and entrepreneurial activity will take off. But any intervention meets a complex reality on the ground: labor regimes that are built around hand cultivation (with specific locally adapted crops); soil that may not respond well to chemical fertilizer; local hearths that may be better suited to diverse quotidian needs; loan and debt systems that march to a different logic; local hierarchies that have long served as mediators of the social and may not rush to embrace new initiatives. I have rarely seen an NGO or government agency that has taken the sociocultural dimension seriously and attribute much of development's failure to that blind spot.

A Brief History of the Kabre

A hill people inhabiting a refuge area where people fled during the era of the Atlantic slave trade (1650–1800), the Kabre developed an ingenious system of terraced cereal farming, which continues into the present. German and French colonial administrators were captivated by Kabre enterprise and conscripted them as laborers in the 1920s to build colonial infrastructure. A decade later, the Kabre began their own migration into sparsely inhabited, albeit fertile, zones in the south of Togo, where they started cash farming cotton, coffee, and cocoa. Their early success and relative autonomy turned a migrant trickle into a stream, producing a steady flow of youth out of the north, an exodus that continues into the present, and established hundreds of Kabre villages across Togo's southern plateau. These emigrants nevertheless have retained strong ties to the north, returning to initiate their children and bury the dead and to remit some of the proceeds of cash-cropping. A busy diaspora emerged around the back-and-forth between northern homeland and southern terminus, crowding the roadways with those heading south in search of money and with southerners returning home for ritual sustenance (Piot 1999: 40–42, 156–71).

Today, youth still head south to work for family members, although Benin and Nigeria to the east have become preferred destinations—both because the southern soil is less fertile than before (and, some say, family members in the south are too exploitative) and because these neighboring countries provide monetary or in-kind remuneration. It is still too early to tell, but if this new migratory trajectory continues (and that to the south diminishes), it will mark something of an epochal transformation in the Kabre social landscape—not only routing migration toward new transnational destinations but also ensuring that youth return to the northern villages after their labor contracts are up (because they are unable to acquire land in Benin and Nigeria). This would repopulate the villages and ensure a greater material return than before while further attenuating ties with family in the south.

Rituals—especially initiation and funeral ceremonies—are a magnet that keeps people returning, tying together Kabre north and south and consolidating identity. In this diasporic context, reciprocity and relational personhood loom large, as "children" in the south retain obligations to family in the north, giving them gifts and showing them "respect" (Piot 1999: 170–71). Here, as with everyday relations among Kabre more broadly and in concert with gift-economy principles, personal relations are forever entangled with the exchange of things (Piot 1999: 52–75).

In the mid-1960s, a Kabre military officer named Gnassingbé Eyadéma, who had fought for the French in Indochina during the late colonial period, took office in Africa's first ever coup and ruled in big-man style until 2005. Eyadéma consolidated power by pivoting national politics around his own ethnic group and by filling the military with soldiers from his natal village. This privileging of birthplace was a constant of Eyadéma's reign—his home village today has paved roads and electricity—but it was accompanied by what many feel was a motivated neglect of surrounding (same-ethnic) villages. Such was certainly the case in Farendé and Kuwdé—the site of the Duke projects today and still a development backwater—and remains a sore spot with locals up to the present, for they had taken Eyadéma in after he was exiled from his natal community (for affairs of witchcraft), and he attended the first mission school in the area before he joined the French army (Piot 2010: 136–38). Uncannily, the Farendé cyber café built by Duke students in 2012 is located on the site of the school Eyadéma attended as a child. These Duke projects might thus be read as inheriting this history of development's promise and neglect.

Student Projects

By any standard, the Kabre villages in northern Togo are materially poor. There is no electricity or running water; houses are covered with thatch or tin; fields are cultivated by hand; poor soil and a harsh climate impede cash-crop cultivation. While weekly markets enable the circulation of local foodstuffs (sorghum, beans, yams, sauce ingredients, chickens, goats), they provide little opportunity for extra income. Moreover, the health challenges in this area of West Africa are legion, with disease a constant in the lives of all. In addition to the tropical fevers—malaria, typhoid, yellow fever—myriad intestinal parasites and worms wreak havoc on bodies and plague the health of families. Up to 50 percent of family income is spent on health care each year.

What can be done in an area like this, especially when virtually all attempts at "development" have failed?

The first thing I tell students is to lower their expectations, even to assume failure—but also that failure can be instructive. The second is to remain open-minded and flexible, always on the lookout for surprises. While some have switched projects altogether in midstream, most have had to innovate along the way, and it is these improvisational moments that have made all the difference. Third, and perhaps most important, I urge students to adopt an attitude of humility toward the local and assume that local knowledge (about crops, soils, markets, health) will trump outsider knowledge most of the time—that one's first instinct should be to find out from villagers how and why they do what they do. I thus insisted that a student who wanted to set up a microfinance initiative in summer 2013 spend her first weeks sitting with women in the market, learning the ins and outs of local payment and debt. When another student became frustrated with inconsistent attendance at the Farendé Writers' Society she had started, I suggested she make the rounds of teachers and students to learn more about attitudes toward literacy. This enabled her to gain empathy for the students and to better strategize ways to increase attendance.

But I feel that the educational process also ought to begin before arriving in the field. Thus, students are encouraged to take courses on African culture and politics and to sign up for an independent study in which they read broadly in anthropological and historical literatures on West Africa and begin to brainstorm their projects. Many of the Togo projects have begun with a research proposal—"I want to study traditional medicines, to determine their effectiveness and to think about ways they might be integrated into clinic practice"—which further gets them into the literature and into a researcher's mind-set. Finally, the fact that eight generations of students have been to the same place means that those who have gone before can share lessons learned with those who follow.

The essays in this book describe the travails of a determined cohort of students—now more than forty, spread over eight years—attempting to initiate small research and development projects that they hope will make a difference. Some have succeeded brilliantly; others are in progress. Still others were unsuccessful and have been abandoned, while some have focused on research more than intervention. One of the most gratifying aspects of this experiment has been its organic nature. From the beginning, it has been a work in progress, one idea and project leading to another, one stray comment or insight opening a new set of possibilities.

The majority of projects, and several featured in this volume, have addressed health—both because of real needs in the villages and because global health is a popular area of study today. Thus, several students have carried out research on the use of vernacular or "traditional" medicines—which proliferate in the villages, where fields are virtual pharmacopeia—trying to better parse local understandings (see chapter 2) and to explore ways in which collaboration between village healers and biomedical clinicians might be brought about (chapter 3). One student (chapter 4) carried the rural medicines project into the capital city, Lomé, where she found that everyone she interviewed—from market women to civil servants—continues to rely on herbal medicine in the treatment of disease (especially in cases of malaria and infertility) and that people often go back and forth between herbalist and clinician.[4]

An ongoing project has been to assess the health insurance system initiated by Duke students in the village of Kuwdé, an initiative that, for all of its apparent benefits, has provided a surprising set of challenges (chapter 5). Conceived by Tara Hopkins, a student in the first cohort in 2008, the insurance scheme offers family coverage—free consultation for all family members and a 75 percent discount on medicine—for only $4 a year. Remarkably, this arrangement has been a financial win-win: families save more money on the medicine they purchase than they spend enrolling, and the clinic makes money from the exchange.[5] One might imagine that, because of the low entry fee, every family in the village would rush to enlist, but at its peak only twenty-three out of two hundred families had signed up, with enrollment dipping to sixteen families in 2013.

A range of reasons appear to account for this puzzling situation. Some of those we asked prefer herbal medicine, which healers dispense free of charge,[6] or they do not trust clinic workers. Others mentioned that having to pay the annual premium on a fixed day (September 1) was burdensome, especially with school fees right around the corner. Yet others said that paying to treat an illness you do not yet have could put you at spiritual risk, potentially bringing on the illness. Moreover, it is important to recognize that the idea of insurance is culturally burdened in ways that render it alien to local sensibilities. The Kabre do not otherwise gamble their money on unknown futures; nor do they pay into a general fund that covers those in need while failing to reimburse those without (but who have already paid in). Put otherwise, the sort of thinking that underlies insurance—hedging against the future, deploying "population" as a category, measuring individuals against statistical (population-level) norms, or what Foucault (2011) calls "biopower"—assumes that people are already inside a distinctively Euro-American cultural order in which the (let's face it, bizarre) logic of insuring one's fate against an unknown future is normalized and becomes a part of the everyday order of things.

In 2013, one of the students began to make some headway in getting people to sign up for the insurance plan by appealing to pecuniary logic. She studied the clinic's books and ran the figures, comparing the expenditures of those who were insured against those who were not (but who still visited the clinic). She then made the rounds of both groups, pointing out to those who were enrolled how much they had saved and to those who were not what they would have saved had they been enrolled. This had an immediate effect, with five new families enrolling within a week. By 2015, forty-seven families were enrolled.

While health remains popular, recent projects have also turned to youth culture. This shift grew out of the research of two students in 2012, Maria Cecilia Romano (chapter 6) and Ben Ramsey, who were interested in the migration of male teens from the villages in Togo to farms in Benin and Nigeria, where they labor for cash or a motorcycle.[7] Local authority figures (parents, chiefs, teachers) have been opposed to this exodus, not only because they lose the labor of their fittest cultivators (and the schools lose students) but also because of the severity of the labor regime in Nigeria and its effects on the health of their children. But teens leave anyway, often sneaking off in the middle of the night, not to return for a year. "We work hard here and have nothing to show for it at the end of the year," they assert. "We work hard in Nigeria, too, but in the end we come back with a motorcycle or a 'video' [TV and DVD player]."

This social drama—which pits children against elders and presages a dramatic shift in local patterns of migration[8]—became the occasion for a set of projects on youth flight. These projects aim not to stem the migratory tide—an impossible task[9]—but seek to make life more palatable for those who remain behind.

The centerpiece of this effort was the installation of a solar-powered Internet café in the village of Farendé. Two students took it upon themselves to design a website where they announced the project and asked for contributions. With the money raised, they purchased laptops and four large solar panels, then shipped them to Togo by express mail. After several near-misses (chapter 7), the equipment arrived, and the two students assembled it all themselves, connecting to the Internet through a local cellphone tower. Now this small village—well off the beaten path, without electricity or the usual amenities—is connected because of a couple of enterprising DIY students.

Aiming to further enhance youth culture in the villages, many of the projects in 2013 were organized around the cyber café. One student offered typing and Internet classes—to which local children flocked—and another created a writers' club (chapter 10). The club used the cyber café as a base of operations, meeting there twice a week to share work (about everyday life in the village), offering students computer access so they could type their essays, and publishing those essays online at the end of the summer (see the website at http://ecrivainsdefarende.wix.com/cljf-2014). Another student set up a microfinance project to lend small sums to teenage boys and girls (chapter 9), the first of its kind in northern Togo, where such loans are usually reserved for adults. She also set up a website that showcased the projects of the four girls and three boys who were funded (http://www.farende.com). A fourth student initiated a project in the mountain village of Kuwdé that enables teenage boys to grow cashew nuts as a cash crop, with the hope that some might find this an attractive alternative to leaving for Nigeria.

While the lines between humanitarian and development aid can blur, and while these projects in Togo have a humanitarian aspect, they technically fall on the "development" side of the charity aid enterprise (Moyo 2009: 7; Redfield 2013: 15). Humanitarian aid is emergency aid—the sort carried out by Médecins sans Frontières in war zones and refugee camps, aiming solely to get people back on their feet—while development aid has a longer view and a commitment to something more than what Peter Redfield (2013: 20) refers to as a "minimal biopolitics." The Duke projects—health insurance, microfinance, the cyber café, computer classes—are intended for the long-term improvement and development of communities.

Despite all of the good intentions and hard work—and the positive feedback students have received—it is worth also considering the complications of installing a cyber café in a village like this. Who will oversee its operation? How much should users be charged so it is affordable while also self-sustaining? How can the equipment be safeguarded? How does one ensure that monies end up in the right pockets? How can one spread computer literacy—typing and Internet skills—in a village where most have never seen a computer before?

A first shock came when we discovered that even at the (seemingly low) user rate of sixty cents an hour, most locals could not afford to use the cyber café. In one month in 2013, it had only three visitors—all adults—and made only fifty cents. A second surprise was that most of the cyber café's income came from charging cell phones (with electricity generated by the solar panels), not from computer use. So this state-of-the-art cyber café had become little more than the village's charging station. There were also whispers that funds were being misappropriated by the young woman who tended the register and by the director. In August 2013, someone broke in at night and made off with three of the laptops.

For all of this, the project still has legs. The thief did not touch the pricier solar panels—which are riveted to the roof—and laptops are easily replaced. A night guard has been hired, and checks against disappearing funds have been put into place. The cyber café now offers free computer access to youth one morning a week, which has begun to create a clientele (chapter 8).

This is how it goes with development: the best-laid plans usually go awry. But it is through setback that such designs become better adapted; that utopian dreams are brought down to earth and retrofitted to the local.

In part I, students reflect on the personal and experiential aspects of living and conducting research in a West African village; part II contains descriptions of some of their projects. Both sets foreground the challenges and surprises that these student-researchers faced and the improvisations they deployed. They should be read together, for the personal-experiential and the formal project forever bleed together in a context such as this. The sets are framed by short essays (an introduction and an epilogue) I wrote to knit together the different initiatives and provide larger context for the project as a whole. What impresses again and again in the students' essays is not only their commitment and hard work, and their willingness to think outside the box, but also that they are not blinded by their idealism. They accept their own and their projects' limitations and are comfortable working within those parameters.

Notes

1. Duke men's lacrosse became national news in 2006 when an exotic dancer, hired to perform at a team party, claimed that she had been raped. While her charge did not stick, the incident remained in the national spotlight for months while claims and counterclaims, and the racial and gendered aspects of the event, were debated and adjudicated. A savvy administration responded to the tarnishing of the university's reputation by, among other things, attempting to rebrand Duke as an institution defined by its "service to society" through establishing programs like DukeEngage.
2. Created in the aftermath of the Duke lacrosse scandal in 2006—and, as suggested above, an attempt to reframe Duke University as more than just a basketball and party school—DukeEngage is a well-endowed program that covers all expenses for students and faculty for more than forty projects worldwide. As of summer 2015, more than three thousand Duke students had volunteered through Duke-Engage in seventy-nine countries on six continents and engaged in more than one million hours of service worldwide.
3. By the early 2000s, both NGOs had departed (par for the course, as NGOs come and go with shocking regularity) and a new microfinance scheme, this one focused on women, had arrived on the scene. In 2012, the state rejuvenated Affaires Sociales—renamed Actions Sociales—and sent a "volunteer" to work in the villages one day a week.
4. Both the United Nations and the World Bank have promoted the enhanced use of "traditional medicine" in countries of the global South, even making it a policy priority, not only because such medicine is cheaper for individuals but also because widespread use will save indebted states significant sums of money that is currently spent on subsidizing pharmaceuticals for their citizens.
5. The clinic charges uninsured patients twice what it pays for medicines and taxes insured patients half what it pays. The clinic makes more money on insurance premiums ($4 per year per family) than it loses in subsidizing the cost of medicines for the insured.
6. While no money changes hands, healers do expect to be "thanked" with a chicken or a small pot of beer by a patient who has been cured by the healer's ministrations. As several interviewees pointed out, the monetary value of this gratuity is far lower than the cost of pharmaceuticals.
7. Girls migrate, too, but in smaller numbers and less often to Nigeria than to Benin, where they work as domestics or in bars. Those who work in the bars often also take up sex work to supplement their meager salaries. Because of the sensitive, locally shameful nature of sex work—due to its health risks and unwanted pregnancies—the students working on youth flight focused more on boys' migratory experiences (but see chapter 6).
8. As mentioned earlier, since the early colonial period (circa 1930), the migratory routes of Kabre youth led to southern Togo, where they cultivated for

family members in return for school fees and pocket change (Piot 1999, 2010). Today, southern money has dried up, and youth are choosing Benin and Nigeria instead. These new destinations have potentially dramatic implications for the northern villages: unlike southern Togo, which often became a terminus where migrant youth would eventually settle, neither Benin nor Nigeria is likely to become a permanent destination, because young migrants have no family or land there. As a consequence, most youth return to the northern villages when their contracts in Benin or Nigeria run out, and with no history or toehold in southern Togo, they typically remain in the north, reversing the trend established during the colonial and early postcolonial periods and potentially also repopulating the villages.

9. There may be few constants across village societies around the world, but the flight of youth is one of them, with the reasons for leaving strikingly uniform: the desire for money, adventure, or a taste of modernity (the "bright lights," in American parlance). Such pull factors are important for Farendé and Kuwdé youth, but they also mention a range of push factors, including the desire to escape authoritarian parents and the excessive demands of family, and the urge to flee what they see as a cauldron of witchcraft to avoid its deadly effects.

References

Benjamin, Bret. 2007. *Invested Interests: Capital, Culture and the World Bank*. Minneapolis: University of Minnesota Press.

Foucault, Michel. 2010. *The Birth of Biopolitics: Lectures at the Collège de France, 1978–1979*. New York: Picador.

Handler, Richard. 2013. "Disciplinary Adaptation and Undergraduate Desire: Anthropology and Global Development Studies in the Liberal Arts Curriculum." *Cultural Anthropology* 28, no. 2: 181–203.

Harvey, David. 2007. *A Brief History of Neoliberalism*. Oxford: Oxford University Press.

Kristoff, Nicholas. 2010. "DIY Foreign-Aid Revolution." *New York Times Magazine*, October 29, 2010.

Moyo, Dambisa. 2010. *Dead Aid: Why Aid Makes Things Worse and How There Is Another Way for Africa*. New York: Farrar, Straus and Giroux.

Piot, Charles. 1999. *Remotely Global: Village Modernity in West Africa*. Chicago: University of Chicago Press.

———. 2010. *Nostalgia for the Future: West Africa after the Cold War*. Chicago: University of Chicago Press.

Redfield, Peter. 2013. *Life in Crisis: The Ethical Journey of Doctors without Borders*. Berkeley: University of California Press.

Part I

Personal Reflections

1. Students Reflect

Stephanie Rotolo, Allie Middleton,
Kelly Andrejko, Benjamin Ramsey,
Maria Cecilia Romano

Stephanie Rotolo

It was barely 5:30 in the morning, but the sun had already begun its ascent, and people and animals were moving about the courtyard. I pushed back the mosquito net that hung above my straw mattress in the corner of the room and slipped my feet out onto the warm clay floor. After a quick, cool bucket shower, I returned to the room, dressed, and ate a breakfast of bean fritters and local beer. I watched and listened as neighbors came and went, conversing in a language I did not understand. I turned off my gas lantern, gathered my notebooks, and gave my Kabre greetings to the women in the courtyard before making my way down the mountain to the small clinic. I passed homesteads and fields along the way and wished everyone I came across a day of productive work.

I was in an entirely different world. I had spent months preparing for this experience—studying the history and culture of the community, practicing my French, and designing my research project—but there were some things I simply could not have anticipated. Effective communication did not just mean speaking a different language; it also required breaking down cultural barriers and being innovative in getting a point across. Time seemed to move at one's own discretion, and what would normally be a ten-minute walk could take up to a half-hour, if, as expected, you stopped to greet the people in your path along the way. Thus, meetings and interviews took place when all participants were present and ready, regardless of the time they had been scheduled. Communication with neighbors required visits to their homes and engaging in face-to-face conversations. The rare cell phones in the village were used for professional purposes or in cases of emergency. Without electricity in the homes, individuals would go to sleep when the sun went down (by 7 PM) and wake up when it rose again (6 AM). Everyone contributed to work around the home and in the fields, and neighbors worked together as one entity for the larger good, redefining the way I perceived "community."

Despite being welcomed by all with an inordinate amount of hospitality, I was still the *anasara* ("Nazarene," in Kabre) or the *yovo* (from the German *jawohl*, in Ewe), the white person. I was stared at by children who had never before seen a foreigner; I was heckled on the streets and in the market; and I was asked countless questions about my life at home and my reasons for coming to this community. A few weeks into my stay, on a Saturday afternoon at a small village market, a woman I did not recognize approached me and told me that I had "saved her." I was confused about what she was referring to; my host brother explained that this was her way to thank me for the health-care discussion I had led the previous weekend. One of the other students and I had decided to host community-wide discussions after Sunday church services to address maternal health, sanitation, and malaria. Apparently, this woman had attended and was adamant in expressing her gratitude for our work in the community.

I had not thought much of it before, but the esteem in which I realized I was being held as a white, foreign student was hard to believe in and get used to. I was told by village chiefs, men's working groups, and other community members how much my work meant to them. While it was certainly comforting to hear this trust, it seemed at times that the community believed more in my capabilities than I believed in myself. In a meeting with the chief of the canton, I was reassured that regardless of what I accomplished during my stay, this experience should be about creating a partnership; that above all, my presence would establish a connection between the villages and a city in my home country.

Most of my days were spent sitting in on consultations at the clinic and conducting interviews, as men took breaks from their long hours of work in the fields. One of the hardest aspects of my research was leaving my preconceptions and personal beliefs at home. As I sought to understand the community's traditional medical system, I delved into entirely unfamiliar topics and issues. Growing up, I was taught that health and disease were simply biological matters, whereas Kabre understood them as interwoven with spiritual and social relations and concerns. With each interview, my previous understandings were twisted and flipped upside down. "Il ne faut pas avoir des inquiétudes," my translator would tell me. "Don't worry." Through the challenges, the fear, and the frustration that inevitably come with cross-cultural experiences, I thought back to what the canton chief had told me when I first arrived in the village about creating a partnership and mutual understanding between cultures. I was there to learn, and I quickly realized that my most enriching experiences would come from asking questions and participating in the local culture as much as possible. I had originally traveled with a research plan in mind, accompanied by particular questions I wanted to ask and issues I thought would be important to discuss with the community. After a somewhat rocky and inhibited start, I finally got comfortable with the interviews—speaking to my translator in French who would then relay information in the local language to the person being interviewed, and vice versa—and allowing them to deviate from what I had intended. I found that doing so gave me greater insight into Kabre culture and opened doors to more questions and areas of research. With few exceptions, people were generally excited about my project. They seemed proud of their culture and wanted to share their personal narratives and insights.

This engagement extended well beyond my formal project. I learned to prepare a local yam dish called *fufu* and made and sold local beer at the nearby market. I played soccer with my host brother and spent hours under the stars in the courtyard playing card games and telling stories with the entire family. I attended ceremonies to the rain spirit, participated in funeral rituals, and spent time in the fields with men's work collectives. By fully immersing myself in Kabre daily life, taking risks and letting go of my fear of failure, I accomplished more than I had imagined and created real relationships that have lasted beyond my stay in northern Togo. The community's unfailing optimism in the face of adversity taught me the value of working through all the challenges with which I am presented, regardless of how insurmountable they may appear at first.

Alexandra Middleton

On my last night in Togo in December 2012, I went to dinner with Dr. Patassi, one of the leading infectious disease physicians in the country, at a restaurant in the capital, Lomé. Patassi, as others call him, is Kabre and lived in the northern villages until he was twenty. He thus grew up using the same local medicines I studied during my fieldwork. Yet he left the villages to pursue biomedical training in Moscow before eventually returning to Lomé to practice. A few minutes into our conversation, I found myself explaining my project to him, telling him about my interest in local healing practices and the challenges of collaboration between biomedical clinics and the House Medical System (HMS) I researched in the north. His response, as I should have anticipated, was skeptical, but it still jolted me: "Why are you interested in that?"

I was thrown in part because his words resonated with those of my premed peers back at Duke who had queried me about my interest in studying non-biomedical forms of healing. In the two years since then, I had chosen not to pursue a career in medicine and instead to explore the anthropology of medical belief and practice, letting go of the idea (of both the doctor in Lomé and my Duke peers) that there might be a single truth by which others might be judged. My fieldwork, and the discourse of medical anthropology I tapped into, allowed me to see such views as epistemic, nested in histories and power plays. Part of my own development—as a thinker, an anthropologist, and a person—required holding on to this insight and moving past stark either-or dichotomies. In this sense, my work evolved with me.

Throughout, the research process for me involved a set of internal negotiations and justifications. Often I questioned whether I would end up contributing anything substantive by the end of my stay. In all honesty, much of the on-the-ground research process struck this very same vulnerable nerve. It frustrated and confused me. Especially at the outset, it felt meandering and unfounded, at times without direction. I quickly learned not to become too attached to any sort of schedule or agenda; at a moment's notice (and sometimes even without notice) it could be felled. Meetings were cancelled and rescheduled; interviewees were often absent or preoccupied with tending their crops and fields.

Furthermore, I quickly grew overwhelmed by the enormity and complexity of the indigenous medical system. I started out with a medical census of sorts but realized that two months would offer barely enough time to scrape the surface. I also realized that the community was reflexively oriented to this deep-rooted medical system and that, as an outsider, I could not expect to immediately understand, navigate, or conceptually inhabit it. Given these circumstances, my work was characterized by constant reassessment and internal questioning, driven by a restless desire to figure out what would best serve the community itself and not just my own intellectual or personal curiosity.

In the midst of these disenchantments, I stumbled upon a partial realization that still continues to play itself out, even as I have returned to the United States. As I relaxed my rigid definition of "change" or "progress," I realized that I would not be able to serve the community unless I really knew it. Even if I struggled to understand or even fully condone the use of local medicines, I *could* at least try to know the community whose lives depended on them. I consciously tried to be more present in my interactions with my family members and the community. I attended all of the ceremonies and funerals that I could. Instead of retiring to my room early, I stayed outside into the night playing cards with the village kids. I brewed the local drink (made by women) with Stephanie and sold it in the Farendé market, much to the delight of my neighbors. When the local musicians played, I applied the few West African dance moves I remembered from the dance class I took during the second semester of my freshman year and joined in the collective movement.

In addition to all of the shifts happening *within* me, I began to notice a shift in the responses of those *around* me. At the beginning, I imagine, the Kabre saw me (understandably) as something of a recluse and as a student who asked strange and seemingly obvious questions about traditional herbs, who stumbled through the local greetings and could hardly carry on a conversation in French. But as I invested more time and energy in my interactions, the divide began to disappear. Even the simple act of stopping on my way down the mountain to engage in a greeting with the toothless old woman who lived outside my homestead yielded smiles and, on my part, a deeper feeling of connection. Welcoming but inevitably detached hospitality morphed into coexistence and laughter.

If I were to attribute this budding intimacy and trust solely to my own efforts, that would be misleading and untrue. Even before I arrived in Kuwdé, a considerable measure of agency and trust was granted by virtue of my professor's rapport with this small community, built on his twenty-five years of fieldwork there. When I entered the village, I received a degree of trust and acceptance that I realize is probably rare in fieldwork and certainly in other areas of international engagement and volunteerism. I was able to ask questions and probe local knowledge in ways that probably would have taken years to establish on my own. For this I felt even more indebted to the community of Kuwdé and even more compelled to contribute something in return.

Since my return, I have repeatedly asked myself: what was the takeaway from my experience in Kuwdé? Among other things, I developed a true appreciation for the fact that change and progress come in modest, often immeasurable amounts. In the middle of an interview, one of the medical workers at the Case de Santé (Health Hut) said, "Thank you for your questions. We learn from them." Our interests as engaged "outsiders" with a desire to learn from the community drive their interests. Our investment in indigenous medicines lend a sort of local legitimacy to the system itself. Our interest in collaboration between the biomedical and local medical practices is, we hope, generating interchange and dialogue between the two, however slowly and subtly.

But on perhaps a more essential level, our presence had an additional effect, however modest. "When you bring your students here, it brings the village to life. No matter what our local struggles, things become sweeter," a village woman told our professor at our farewell ceremony. That sweetness (happiness?) is perhaps the most resonating affect I will take away from my time in Kuwdé. It is a different flavor from any I have seen or experienced in my life to this point. It is founded in people, not in acquisitions or individual accomplishments, money or hedonistic pleasures. It is the toothless smile of the old lady after I greet her in her own tongue, the euphoric giggle of a young child chirping from the tall grasses as I return a *bonjour*. In this place where survival and health are not one's own business but the business of an entire village, exchange and interchange yield the most enduring sense of fulfillment, purpose, and vitality.

Kelly Andrejko

The first day I set foot in the Hôpital du Bè, in Lomé, Togo's capital, my heart was about to beat out of my bright blue scrubs. I had just zoomed to the hospital on only my third motorcycle ride ever, and it felt as if all eyes in Lomé were on me. I took a deep breath and reminded myself why I was standing in the sweltering heat of an African summer, in the waiting room of an urban Togolese hospital. I had received a grant from Duke to travel to Togo's capital for eight weeks the summer after my sophomore year to conduct research about the intersection between biomedical and tradi- tional medicine, as well as to shadow health professionals at the hospital. Nevertheless, all of the confidence I had conveyed in my grant proposals seemed to be evaporating as I looked around for the director of personnel with whom I was to check in. Quickly scanning the room, sweating bullets, I saw a person screaming with a green and furry infection on his leg. *No, not him*, I thought. I saw an authoritative-looking nurse in a striped red outfit glaring at me. *No, not him.* Then I saw a smiling man in white lab coat head- ing my way. *That's him!*

The day before, in a comfortably air-conditioned director's office, it had been carefully explained that my fellow Duke student, Camille, and I would be spending two weeks in each of the hospital's main units—gynecology, pediatrics, and general medicine—leaving the remaining two weeks up to us. Day one for me was a trip to the *sale d'accouchement* (birthing room).

As I was dropped off in the birthing room, I quickly remembered that my shadowing experience back home had been confined to the consul- tations of a pediatric neurologist, all neat and bloodless. I was instantly overwhelmed as I stepped into the stuffy, poorly ventilated birthing ward. Momentarily struck speechless by the birth occurring on one of five cloth- covered metal tables directly in front of me, I was broken out of my stupor by a midwife handing me a pair of gloves and a face mask and instructing me to take over for her. In my rusty French, I sputtered that I was there just to observe; I was not trained in any way to help with birthing. This would be a conversation I would have dozens more times at the hospital that sum- mer, as no one could understand why I would travel to a hospital in urban Africa with no medical training. Saying no was one of the most difficult parts of my work at the hospital, as the doctors were clearly overwhelmed with patients, yet I knew I did not have the necessary knowledge to be of use. In the birthing ward, the midwife looked utterly confused until the lady in the stall next to us started screaming in Ewe, the local language, that her baby was coming, and the midwife signaled for me to follow along.

Before I knew it there was a baby, washed and swaddled and placed on a counter in a side room; the midwife had again moved on, asking whether I wanted to feel intervaginally for the positioning of the baby in our next patient. As I adamantly shook my head no, I felt my old-school Nokia phone buzz in my front pocket. It was a text from Camille, who had been placed in a room mysteriously labeled "Small Surgeries." "How do you say 'throw-up' in French?" she wrote. All of the excitement in the birthing ward had left me a little queasy, and I was slightly relieved to know I was not the only one having difficulty adjusting to the extreme heat and pungent smell. Unfortunately, I was replying to the text at the exact moment the hospital's head of gynecology, whom the director of personnel could not locate earlier that morning for a proper introduction, chose to walk into the unit. With a scathing glare, she demanded to know who I was and what kind of professional I was, using a cell phone in her suite. I carefully tried to explain I was an American, there to conduct research and observe in the hospital, while my friend was sick in another service and did not speak much French, and . . . She cut me off with a glare, informed me again that phone use was unacceptable, and hurried off. At that point, I just hoped I would make it to lunch.

Luckily, my shadowing got much easier after the first day. For starters, I quickly discovered that the surgery and recovery rooms for C-sections were air-conditioned, and when I needed a break from the heat, the surgeons were more than happy to have someone to share their space with. As an added bonus, the efficiency, precision, and teamwork with which the surgeons worked was incredibly fun to watch tableside. So accustomed to the Health Insurance Portability and Accountability Act (HIPAA) laws back home, I was shocked that no patients were ever asked whether it was OK for me stand next to the operating table or to learn details about their private medical histories. The decisions of the surgeons in the hospital never appeared to be questioned directly by the patients, and as I was Caucasian and wearing scrubs (I honestly could not tell which mattered more), I was considered one of them.

My favorite days were spent in the cardiology clinic, held every Friday in a closet of a room used by a psychiatrist for the HIV/AIDS patients on all other days of the week. That cardiology was my favorite came as a bit of a surprise to me, as I had no prior knowledge of or interest in the heart. Nevertheless, during mornings from day one the nurses entrusted me with taking the weights and histories of new patients. Although these were tasks of small importance, I always felt as if a great responsibility had been put on my shoulders—and was forever concerned, despite the reassurance of the nurses, that a piece of important information would be lost in my hesitant French transcription.

After the files for the day were complete, I would slip back to the consultation room to observe the patients' visits with the doctor. The cardiologist who staffed the weekly clinic was very young and energetic—a necessity, as he could see up to seventeen patients in the three hours he was at the hospital. The doctor was not bashful, either: after explaining to me that the local diet, which was very heavy in carbohydrates and oil, was responsible for the majority of obesity cases we were seeing, he exclaimed to a female patient, "You're too fat! I bet you crush your husband in bed!" It soon became painfully obvious that being a cardiologist in a poor country was challenging in ways that would be unimaginable in the United States. The hospital had no equipment for him to use: no electroencephalogram (EEG), no ultrasound, and some days even the blood pressure cuff was broken. Although he could prescribe medicine for his patients and make referrals to other clinics for tests, very few of them could actually afford anything aside from basic treatment because of the lack of insurance. While he would try to explain the importance of a balanced diet and daily exercise, he admitted that very few people would actually be able to make the necessary changes. Nevertheless, I was incredibly inspired by his work, coming back week after week, seeing the same patients, and trying to make whatever difference he could.

After the first two weeks spent getting my feet on the ground in the hospital, I began to use the afternoons to conduct interviews, both in the hospital and around town, for my research project. Almost all of my interviews had to be conducted with a local translator, as many people did not speak adequate French, and, as I quickly learned, my white skin created a cultural barrier that was often difficult to overcome. Even if the person I was speaking with spoke French, the presence of someone local helped the interviewee lose initial inhibitions. When conducting interviews throughout the city, I would often be invited into households and offered the only seat and whatever refreshments the family had to provide. Similar to being at the hospital, most seemed confused about why I had chosen to come to Togo. "Peace Corps?" was a common question.

Nevertheless, everyone seemed to have something to say once I started asking for his or her opinion on health care. For some, the hospital represented the optimum standard of care—of European medicine and tests that were infallible. One of the most insistent and unexpected patrons of biomedical care I found was an older grandmother whose daughter had gone to medical school in Europe; subsequently, the *grand-mère* relied solely on the medicine her daughter mailed back. Others were quicker to mention the hospital's shortcomings—long waiting times, irritable doctors, and, of course, the cost. Most who leaned toward "traditional" routes for care were eager to get my opinion, to find out what I thought of these medicines. Just as I had my own stereotypes of them, they had theirs of me, assuming I looked down on traditional medicine—like all Americans, they imagined. For some, it was a surprise that I was attempting to be neutral about the issue.

Some of my favorite interviews were with the traditional medical practitioners. While I had conducted a lot of background research on the topic before the trip, interacting directly with these healers was what allowed me to see firsthand the many benefits of herbal medicine. My first interview with a healer, conducted a week into the trip, made the strongest impression on me. My translator and I really hit the jackpot when we knocked on the door of a shop in an area known to be a permanent place of business for many healers. Peeking our heads in, we saw a middle-aged woman reclining on a mattress to avoid the heat, surrounded by bottles of meticulously labeled natural products. She graciously offered us the only two chairs in the room and asked how she could help. As I explained my project and outlined the questions I had for her, she smiled and started to tell the story of the origins of her interest in medicine, listing reasons that sounded remarkably similar to my own. She became interested in traditional medicine as a child in southwestern Togo; while hanging out around the older healers, she would write down their cures in a little notebook so she could play healer when her own family members were ill. As she grew older, she received a formal three-year education in Benin; at this point in her story, she proudly pulled out her *diplome d'aptitude à la pratique de médicine traditionelle* and *diplome de pharmacologie* for us to examine. After spending time practicing in Benin, and then in Gabon, she returned to her homeland and set up the practice she runs today. Most of the patients she sees hear about her by word of mouth, following a diagnosis at the hospital and seeking supplementary or cheaper treatment. The majority of her patients visit for help with sexually transmitted diseases and infertility; as an example, she showed me a white powder, explaining that it should be mixed with food to increase the viability of sperm. The interview continued on in this vein for the next hour, as she carefully explained the inventory of her shop and how each plant was picked, dried, and crushed, then tested on herself for toxicity. I found it incredible there could be no labs, no government support, and no advertising, yet her business thrived.

For me, these stories of autonomy, determination, and tradition strongly embodied what I found to be the Togolese spirit of medicine. In a cardiology clinic where a Togolese doctor challenges tradition to get his patients to adapt their dietary habits or in the office of a traditional healer who embraces it, I observed how local medicine became a constant balance between the two practices. As the two categories of physicians existed independently of each other, they encountered many different challenges in their daily practices. Nevertheless, both clearly demonstrated their belief that they had the best interests of their patients in mind.

Benjamin Ramsey

I remember first hearing, during my childhood in France, about Médecins sans Frontières and how it sends doctors to crisis locations around the world. It seemed cool to think that a career of helping people might also be an adventure. Later, in high school, I was tugged in the same direction by the documentary *Invisible Children*. The film's directors, three college students from California, dropped into Uganda planning to document the war in Darfur but instead encountered child soldiers. I wanted to be like those students. I wanted to make a difference. I became active in my high school's Invisible Children club, but by the time I entered college, I was tired of simply fundraising. After reading Tracy Kidder's *Mountains beyond Mountains*, I became interested in the idea of health care as a human right, a more concrete version of the Invisible Children's principle that "where you live shouldn't determine whether you live." I wanted to be on the ground, ensuring that my time and effort were truly making a difference. Despite the presence of significant health inequalities here at home, I wanted to make a difference abroad, outside my comfort zone. My excuse to myself was that those in developing countries need help more than Americans. And I wanted to go to an "exotic" locale, where I could be of help.

"Ben's going to Africa this summer!" Africa. No, not Togo. Africa. How could my family or I have had expectations of Togo, when none of us had even located the country on a map until we heard of Duke's Togo program? For all I knew beforehand, Togo could have been in the Caribbean. I chose to pursue going to Togo only because of the program's connection with global health and the fact that Togo is Francophone. My only experience with Africa prior to Togo consisted of reading books such as *Heart of Darkness* and *Things Fall Apart* and viewing Hollywood films such as *Blood Diamond*, *The Last King of Scotland*, and *Hotel Rwanda*. Africa for me was a wilderness full of pickup trucks bearing blood-thirsty, machine gun-wielding warlords. Africa was rampant with corruption and crises. Africa was thirsty, and this thirst could be quenched even by a freshman college student.

After arriving in Togo, our group of students spent several days getting oriented in Lomé. I remember noticing large lizards crawling all over the place, like squirrels back home. I saw how all buildings, even the least wealthy, were built of concrete. And, of course, I was amazed at the relative absence of white Europeans and Americans—and of the resulting awkward eye contact with other expatriates. I was excited to head north by the time we loaded up in my professor's car for the day-long trip. But why was I so eager to get out of the capital? I wanted to see the "real" Africa. I had explicitly chosen not to stay in the capital, instead wanting to spend the summer in a rural village with no running water or electricity.

As the weeks went by, I began to truly enjoy my summer. I learned to love rain—the way it cooled things down and its sound on my tin roof. As the corn and sorghum stalks grew, I became closer with my neighbors and familiar with faces at the market. I started to genuinely appreciate the people, how even in an area as poor as the village where I lived people were full of life and energy. As I met more and more individuals and became, albeit superficially, a part of the community, I began to imagine how villages of people, just like the one in which I lived, are what make up developing countries. My personal relationships reinforced my desire to make a difference. Developing countries were no longer dots on the global map in high school history class. These global inequalities affect life at the individual, personal level.

I now realize how naïve I was in my reasons for going to Togo. Although I still enjoy visiting countries for the first time, adventure is much less of a factor in my pursuit of a career in global health. The personal relationships I formed while I was in Togo tore apart my Western stereotypes of Africa. In my mind, Africa is no longer a wild backdrop for crises and corresponding do-gooders. Africa is full of individuals—individuals just like my host parents and siblings.

Maria Cecilia Romano

I arrived in Lomé at twilight in early May. I remember looking out of the window of the plane and immediately registering that I was not flying into a glittering national capital. Instead of the familiar highways of red and white and the sprawling seas of winking lights, I saw a vast expanse of rusty brown, dotted with trees and what seemed to be small fires in the distance. The pinks and oranges in the sky were quickly fading to deep purples and blues, and before I knew it the door of the plane was opening. A wave of overwhelmingly warm, sticky, and humid air billowed in. "Welcome to Togo!" I had no idea what adventures awaited me, no way to know that the next two months would be the most formative, fulfilling, and memorable of my life to date.

In our now entirely too warm sweatpants and sweatshirts, two other Duke students and I were challenged in navigating the Gnassingbé Eyadéma International Airport—not because it was big but because our failure to pay the immigration officers a bribe meant we were the last in the crowd of people to receive our visas. Finally, we were handed back our passports, and we walked outside to meet the smiling faces of Professor Piot, who later insisted we call him Charlie, and Fidèle, a young and vibrant woman who acted as our guide in Lomé and friend throughout the trip. Soon we were joined by the other four students on the program, and after a few days of orientation and supply purchasing, and many Youki soft drinks, fried plantains, and "Lomé salads" (a specialty dish made with lettuce, pasta, eggs, and mayonnaise) later, five of us headed to the north, where we would be conducting research and living with host families in the villages of Kuwdé and Farendé.

The drive to the north was a long seven hours of dusty, bumpy roads, but when we finally arrived, I was taken aback by the beauty around me. As it was the rainy season, the tall grasses in the plains and the enormous teak tree leaves were electric green with new life. We lugged our backpacks up the rocky trail to Kuwdé, and after the sacrifice of a white chicken to honor our arrival, we all ended up in someone's homestead drinking *sulum*, the local beer, out of hollowed-out calabashes. A growing crowd of terrified yet curious children, enthusiastic teens, men tired from cultivating all day, and old women wearing far fewer items of clothing than I am used to seeing poured in to greet us with a friendly *Alafea wei!* ("how's your health?"). I felt like I was in a movie or a picture from my seventh-grade social studies textbook. I was mentally and physically exhausted, yet exhilarated and eager to start learning everything I could about this beautiful and mysterious place.

My intention is not to distort or romanticize. There were definitely things that took time to get used to: the spicy food that seemed to turn my stomach inside out; the fact that I had to brush my teeth with bottled water to avoid getting sick; the many, many, many varieties of bugs that liked to visit my room; the periodic torrential downpours; the heat; the cold bucket showers; and the lack of electricity all reminded me how strange this place was compared with my home back in the United States.

But soon the strange began to seem familiar and the familiar, strange. I stopped reaching for the nonexistent light switch when entering my room at my homestay; I learned to wash my clothes by hand; and I became accustomed to waking up at sunrise and going to sleep soon after sunset. By contrast, encounters with commonplace luxuries such as SUVs, ice (and cold things in general), and toilets became entirely out of the ordinary. It even became jarring to encounter other Caucasians. "Seriously, what are they doing here?" we would ask in unison whenever we saw other foreigners in nearby Kara or at "our" market in Farendé. I gained a new mom, a new grandmother, five new sisters, and five new cousins—a family that stole my heart and with whom I keep in touch to this day. People in the village began to greet me by my Kabre name, Essosolom, which means "liked by God," and I learned enough of the local language to be able to greet them back. I also became passionate about my research within the community, and as people came to learn what I wanted to study and why, many went out of their way to support my efforts. Even though the excited choruses of

"*Anasara! Anasara!* Bye, bye!" (White person! White person! Goodbye!) from village children never really subsided, I slowly began to forget that I did not belong there, and Farendé became my home, a home I hope to return to one day soon.

For my research, I knew I wanted to explore the migration of youth out of the village, but I had no idea *how* exactly I would do that. I had read some material about fieldwork methods before I arrived, but I mostly learned by doing. The following are some of the most crucial lessons I learned about field research. I have tried to include only those that might be universally applicable and not location-specific, but they will be most relevant for students doing research in small communities with whose culture and language they are unfamiliar. Half of the fun was figuring these things out for myself, but I hope that these musings might still be helpful for other students living in new environments and conducting community-based research for the first time.

1. *Learn everything you can about the location you will be in.* This should include the predominant ethnic groups and religions, the government structure and leadership, the current economic situation, cultural norms, the health care and education systems, and anything else you can get your hands on. Even if it does not seem immediately relevant to your research topic, you will be surprised at how interconnected all of these things are. For me and the other students I traveled to Togo with, it was helpful to take an independent study with our professor the semester preceding our trip, but in retrospect I still wish I had researched even more before arriving. The more you know, the better off you will be. Your background knowledge will help put things into context once you start gathering information. If you will not have frequent access to a computer, consider printing out some literature that you can refer back to when necessary.

2. *Make an effort to learn the local language.* Learn what you can beforehand, and once you arrive continue to ask people to teach you key words and phrases. Stop worrying about getting things wrong and sounding foolish. Practice with locals. You will improve faster *and* it will mean a lot to them that you are trying. In fact, people are likely to be more willing to help you and answer your questions. If you hear the same words come up again and again in interviews or conversations around you, ask what they mean. Ask how to say things you wish you could convey to people, even if it is just

"This *fufu* is delicious" or "How was the market?" or "No, I am not married (or looking to be married)." A little genuine effort can go a long way. It can make all the difference.

3. *Put some thought into your research design.* A useful way to start is by producing a map—a strategy by which you ask multiple people in your community, young and old, men and women, to help you "map out" the village, highlighting the location of schools, hospitals, and other public infrastructure; water sources; different religious or ethnic groups; the homes of important people; main roads; marketplaces; and whatever else they deem important. The objective is to get a sense of how life works in your community, how and where people interact, who has access to which resources, and so on. If your research design includes interviews, make sure you talk to a representative sample, including people in minority groups and people who live in far corners of your village that are difficult to get to. You do not want repetitive information from a homogenous group. Strive to learn about your topic from many different viewpoints. You will learn more, and your research will be more accurate, even if the complexity means the data take longer to analyze and understand.

4. *Foster a good relationship with your translator.* If you are working with a translator, put time and energy into getting to know him or her, even if you do not become the best of friends. The quality of information you are able to get will reflect this effort. Get a sense for where he or she comes from and what kinds of biases he or she might have based on class, ethnicity, religion, political affiliation, and so on. Ask yourself how this might affect your interviews with certain people and plan accordingly. In general, it is useful to just be aware of these potential biases so that you can separate opinions he or she might express from more objective information. Remind your translator that you want him or her to *translate*, not interpret. At the end of the interview, you can ask about his or her opinions, impressions of the interviewee, whether he or she trusted the information given, and any other questions you have. Take what the translator says with a grain of salt, but this commentary is often useful and very interesting. Further, the translator's job is an extremely difficult one, so be aware of how he or she is doing and take breaks as needed, especially if you are working in a difficult environment.

5. *Set up interviews in advance.* If there are specific individuals you want to speak to, seek them out and ask to schedule a convenient time to return

and interview them. Be mindful of the fact that people are busy with their daily tasks and will not always be ready or willing to be asked questions when it happens to be convenient for you. If they are willing to talk to you right away, make sure they know how much time the interview will take.

6. *Speaking of time, do not expect people to show up on time, or at all.* Indians call this "Indian standard time"; Thai people call it "Thai time"; and the Togolese call it "West Africa time." Being late is not seen as, or intended to be, disrespectful; it is just a cultural difference. Sometimes things come up in people's daily lives that are more urgent than the interview they promised you. Perhaps your translator has a family emergency that he or she needs to take care of before helping you. Be flexible. Do not despair. Keep trying.

7. *Build rapport.* Put yourself in your interviewee's shoes. If a stranger came into your house and started asking you potentially invasive questions about your life, health, family, or other things, you would probably be a little hesitant. Make sure you introduce yourself and explain why you are doing the work you are doing and how you will keep your subject's responses confidential. People might not want to talk to you. Respect that. If they do, make sure they feel comfortable with you. Start out by asking them about themselves, their family, and what they do; then continue into your actual research questions. Know that people might not tell you the truth, especially about sensitive issues. Getting to the bottom of things might require triangulation of information with other people in the village or a re-interview, or both. Have patience.

8. *Be honest.* If you do not think the results of your research will help your interviewee or his or her community directly, immediately, or at all, do not lie and say they will. It is common to be asked questions such as, "Why are you asking me this?" or "How will this help me?" In these situations, I remember immediately feeling terrible about what I was doing and useless because I did not have the power, resources, or depth of knowledge to really fix the problem I was learning about. My professors and mentors have since advised me not to feel bad or ashamed but simply to explain to my interviewees that I am a student and that I am trying to learn from *them* and their community. Be sure to break down any misconception that you are better or smarter or more able than your interviewees. They have knowledge about a particular problem you are interested in learning more about. Do not belittle them or let them belittle themselves. Sometimes I like to add that it is my hope to one day know enough about this topic

to be able to inform policymakers directly or indirectly in their efforts to address it.

9. *Prepare to hear things that might be upsetting.* I had to hold back tears once as a woman in Farendé told me that six of her eleven children had died and the other five had migrated and left the village. Her youngest daughter left with a hustler when she was eleven and was "treated like a slave" and sexually abused by her employer until she was found and brought back to the village. Every situation is different, so there is no uniformly tactful way to handle difficult situations, but putting down your pen and notebook, looking your interviewee in the eyes, and showing your sincere empathy is always a good place to start.

10. *Let people ask you questions.* My favorite part of interviews, and something I highly recommend, is to conclude by letting interviewees ask me questions. I tell them the questions can be about anything—my life, culture, home, school, and so on. Expect them to be curious and be ready to be honest. After all, the experience should not be one-sided. You should offer, not just extract, information. This is sometimes informative and often hilarious. In field interviews I have been asked why I and "my people" are so white, where the water in my home comes from, and why I am not married yet. (I am currently twenty-one.) The questions asked really show what that person cares about and speak to her or his worldview.

11. *Write everything down—gut reactions, questions to ask later, and suddenly lucid insights.* I know I personally forget these things if I do not, so I always, ALWAYS have pen and paper handy. Try to write about your findings intermittently and adapt the entries as you continue to learn more. Getting your preliminary conclusions down on paper early on will help you identify holes in your research, questions to which you still need answers, and ways to proceed. If possible, type up and organize your fieldwork and interview notes at the end of every day while they are still fresh. This way, things that you remember from your interactions but may have forgotten to jot down will still be in your memory. I also recommend keeping a personal journal. Your experiences will be so new and different—and, at times, overwhelming—that you will need a way to reflect.

12. *Consider collecting both qualitative and quantitative data.* I got the most information out of my qualitative interviews, but in the end I realized that I really wanted to know the quantitative scope of youth migration from Farendé, so I did a door-to-door survey of a percentage of the homes in each

of the three sectors of the village to try to map out how many young people (age nine to twenty-five) had left in the previous five years, where they had gone, and for what purpose. This information is often painstaking to collect, but it allows you to make numerical comparisons, chart and graph information, and examine your findings in a different way. The analysis of your quantitative information can also inform or change the questions you ask in subsequent interviews.

13. *Make use of useful people.* If someone is particularly friendly or helpful, accept her or his support. A reliable contact who knows the community well is invaluable. He or she is likely to be an important source of information, but even if the individual does not have the specific answers you are looking for, he or she can probably put you in touch with someone who does. Having a local on your side also shows others in the community that you can be trusted.

14. *Du courage.* Sometimes it will be too rainy or too cold or too hot or too windy or too bug-infested to conduct interviews effectively. Sometimes people will be hard to find or uncooperative. Sometimes crying babies or meddlesome goats or other things will get on your nerves and make it hard to hear and think straight during interviews. Do not get discouraged. In the end, you will be proud of how you have pushed yourself. All the same, be kind to yourself. There is only so much you can get done in a week, two months, four months, or even a year. Distinguished academics spend whole decades studying single communities and are still learning new things. Setting unachievable goals will make you very unhappy. Follow your gut and follow your leads. If you encounter something strange or something you do not understand, ask about it. Then ask some more, or ask someone else. There is a solution to most every obstacle.

15. *Respect cultural norms.* If it is not appropriate to go out after dark, or consume alcohol, or wear shorts, or wear shoes inside certain places, do not. Women especially must take care to dress and act appropriately, as different cultures have very different notions of what is and is not culturally acceptable for women to do and wear. Sometimes it is frustrating, but ignoring these cultural guidelines could have serious repercussions in regard to your work and your relationships with people in the community. It is also very easy to be judgmental about things that are culturally acceptable— among other things, corporal punishment, child marriages, polygamy, and four-year-olds drinking beer with total impunity. Be as open-minded as

possible and put your own cultural biases aside. You are not there to pass judgment on people; you are there to learn from them.

16. *Take part in community activities and remember to have fun.* Your experiences outside interviews and formal research can be equally enriching. Play soccer or traditional games with children and other young people. Attend marriages and funerals and other religious ceremonies and rites of passage. Try cultivating in the fields, or pounding yams into *fufu*, or carrying water from the well on your head, or sweeping the courtyard with a bundle of reeds, or whatever else might make up daily life in your research community. Share your culture, too. Show pictures of your family; cook food for people to try; let them listen to your music. Remember that you are representing your culture: the people you encounter probably will never have interacted with someone like you. One of my favorite moments of living in my homestay in Farendé occurred when I cooked chocolate cake for my host family. The Togolese diet does not include sugar, and they went nuts for my Nutella, M&Ms, and candle-covered masterpiece. We had a great time figuring out how to cook it within the limitations, which included the lack of a real oven.

17. *Give back.* Even if I could not solve the problems of youth migration, child labor, and child trafficking, I wanted to leave the village better off in some way. I did not want to leave people wondering and asking what, exactly, I had been doing in their midst. Even more so, I did not want them to feel as if I had taken their life stories and personal information and simply disappeared. We decided to organize a conference about youth migration and to include teachers, parents, young men and women, chiefs, religious leaders, and others we had spoken to during our two-month stay. The idea was to give everybody a chance to voice their opinions and learn from one another and from our findings. Although the conference may not have gone exactly as intended (there was sensitive information that people were unwilling to discuss publicly), I think it brought to light an important issue and got people thinking and talking about how they could address youth migration as a community. In addition, I decided to donate the laptop and a solar panel I had bought with my grant money to be used jointly by three groups in the community that work toward village development, women's issues, and education. I also left a written report of my findings in French so people could read about what I had been able to discover. Your contribution can be anything you see fit. Organize a meeting, a dinner, a dance,

or even an exhibition of pictures you have taken. Show members of the community what you have learned from them, and take the opportunity to thank them.

Working in Togo was one of the best experiences of my life. I pushed myself to adapt to a completely foreign environment and really came to love my new home. I grew a lot as a person and made friendships that I truly treasure. It was rewarding to study a topic that was important to this community, and one that few have really explored at the micro-level of a single village. I loved my first taste of research in the field so much that I went on to do very similar work in India and China. I would encourage anybody to take advantage of a similar opportunity, and my advice, in sum, is to have fun and to not get discouraged by the many challenges you will encounter. Your perseverance will be well worth it in the end.

Part II

Research Articles

2. The Social Life of Medicine

Alexandra Middleton

Even at the earliest hours of the day, you are bound to encounter someone on the network of paths linking the homesteads of the mountain village of Kuwdé who will greet you with a series of questions (to which you
will provide answers). The exchange can be as short as a few seconds or as
long as several minutes. Beginning with a predictable structure, it spirals
into nuance, picking up rhythm and tempo, adding a musical quality to
the already lyrical Kabre language. Almost like a dance, the lead shifts; the
questioner becomes the respondent. Your participation in this exchange
signifies intimacy and an understanding of local protocol. Indeed, it took
me several weeks to keep in step without fumbling and faltering.

Yet more intriguing than this iterative ritual, or even the questions
posed, are the answers given in response. As diverse as the questions may
be, a single word often suffices: *alafia*. A Kabre word probably derived from
Hausa,[1] *alafia* means "health" or "well-being." Here is a rough translation of
what one might consider the core of a Kabre greeting exchange:

You have come?
Eh (Yes).
You and the morning/midday sun/evening/night [depending on time of
  day]?
Alafia-we (Health is).

In your work?
Alafia-we (Health is).
Your home?
Alafia-we (Health is).
Your market?
Alafia-we (Health is).
Your fields?
Alafia-we (Health is).
Your family?
Alafia-we (Health is).

If language reflects culture, then this exchange holds telling clues as to the centrality of health for the Kabre and to the multiple ways in which it is conceived. More than a placeholder or utterance, alafia becomes the answer to myriad personal and community-wide questions, a subject of public concern. Its presence quells worries; its absence raises discord. Health, in Kuwdé, is the business of the entire village.

I began to realize that this metaphor—health as the business of a village—asserted its presence in more ways than one, and I became interested in how this notion of health as a community concern played out, particularly in the local medical system. My interviews and discussions revealed an intricate network of medicines purposefully distributed among houses in Kuwdé. Born into this "house medical system," Kabre individuals are naturalized within a social fabric; remedies become yet another way to orient oneself to kin and clan. The act of health seeking puts bodies into relationship with houses, community members, and ancestors. The association of certain houses with their remedies entwines with local knowledge and history. Within this democratized form of medicine, as the healer Kouwènam put it, "everyone is a healer."

I had not always intended to study this topic. I had arrived in Kuwdé with a foggy, largely academic notion of "traditional medicine." Along with a suitcase and small backpack, I had brought a roughly defined research question with me to Togo, more affiliated with the field of global health than with that of anthropology. I initially intended to focus on the relationship between the Western biomedical clinic in Kuwdé—the Case de Santé (Health Hut)—and the "traditional" medical system. I hoped to identify potential areas of collaboration and cross-pollination between the two.

Subjects such as these tend to captivate global health research, particularly driven by recent international interest in complementary and alternative medicine. I saw my fieldwork as a contribution to this discussion, focusing specifically on a region of Togo that had not previously been examined through this lens.

Yet just as I felt initially disoriented—even paralyzed—by the Kabre greeting exchange, I quickly realized I had little idea what "traditional medicine" meant in the context of Kuwdé. Even supposing that such a system existed as a singular entity proved problematic, especially when the "system" I sought to discover revealed itself as multimodal, layered, and unbounded. I soon discovered that the system extended far beyond remedies and their applications into the realm of relationships among people, histories, and futures.

Positioning and Framing

When considering the local, indigenous, "traditional" healing practices of non-Western societies, Euro-Americans often ask whether they are efficacious—"Do they work?" (Kirmayer 2004: 42). This question captivates the imagination and interest of those rooted in the biomedical tradition. Research into ethnomedicine aims to test the biological efficacy of certain herbal treatments, and interest in cross-systems integration drives research of drug-herb interactions. But from a biomedical perspective, our conception of "work" tends to be narrowly defined. Are the remedies efficacious? Do they heal? Do they *work*? We seek to assign a value of worth based on whether treatments cure or ameliorate the physical symptoms of disease and sickness. But just as medicine is an intensely context-specific, culturally embedded practice, the term "work"—and the way that we conceive of it—begs greater nuance. Asking "what, how, and why" a practice works requires a simultaneous exploration of what Laurence Kirmayer calls "basic or anterior questions": "what it *means* for something 'to work', what it is supposed to be working *on*, and toward *what end*" (Kirmayer 2004: 46). Work, in this sense, is inextricably linked to power, meaning, and context.

This essay challenges and expands the ways in which we might think about the "work" performed by a so-called traditional medical system. Using Kabre medicine as a lens, I challenge fixed notions of work, the body, tradition, medicine, and health. I aim to move from a conception of health solely as biological pathway to situating health in its social and relational dimensions. Applying the question of "work" to the Kabre medical system, I will show that a medical system does social, relational, and political work, as well as physiological "work."[2] That is, it not only knits together homesteads and lineages through a precisely articulated division of medical knowledge and practice but also provides relief—bodily and relationally—in the face of illness. I argue that an expanded notion of efficacy, informed by local practice, may improve global health work. The critical issue remains cultivating awareness of how definitions of efficacy frame the lived experience and practice of medicine in northern Togo and, in turn, of health.

Methodology and Terminology

I conducted my fieldwork during the summer of 2011, from the months of June to August, and for two weeks in December 2012 in Kuwdé. In addition to carrying out my independent research, I attempted to integrate myself into the village of Kuwdé the best I could, attending ceremonies and funerals, brewing sorghum beer and selling it in the marketplace along with other Kabre women, and helping the local biomedical clinic deliver public health messages about mosquito net use, hygiene, and prenatal checkups for expectant mothers.

Nearly thirty semi-structured interviews with local Kabre healers, along with informal discussions with community members and a two-day collaborative conference between biomedical and traditional healers, inform this work. Field notes were either handwritten or tape-recorded and transcribed. I returned to Kuwdé nearly a year and a half after I first left to double-check my initial understandings of the local medical system and to pose questions previously off my radar, questions that arose from months of ruminating, poring over field notes, and writing. As a fieldworker, returning to one's field site poses a great risk; there is always a chance you will discover that you completely misinterpreted or misrepresented your subjects and topic of study. While my return interviews expanded and enhanced my understanding of medical beliefs and practices in Kuwdé, I was relieved to find that my initial interpretations were largely confirmed, even resoundingly so, in follow-up conversations.

I conducted my interviews with the help of two interpreters: Jesper and Georges. Without them, this work would have proved impossible, as I had a rather cursory knowledge of French and an even more limited familiarity with Kabre. The process of translation is fraught with complication, especially in ethnographic research. Integral components get lost or misconstrued, even among the most skilled interpreters, due to inherent differences of syntax, idiom, and expression of meaning. The production of this work, from its inception to its current state, was a dance of three languages: Kabre, West African French, and English. Often, my field notes appeared to be a jumbled mélange of Kabre, French, and English words. To address the limitations and borders of my interpretations, I employ a first-person narrative. I do so to acknowledge the dissonance and disjuncture—and the inherently subjective nature—of the interviewing and interpreting process.

Linguistic variability and nuance not only relate to the politics of translation; the language we use to speak about or depict culture itself proves delicate. Each word carries with it particular baggage. A litany of terms has emerged to define or classify medical systems *other* than Western biomedicine, including "traditional," "indigenous," "vernacular," "ethno-," and "folk." One cannot underestimate the power of the current moment in influencing this discourse. For instance, centuries' worth of herbal remedies, acupuncture, massage, and dietary practice, among others, have been synthesized and systematized into the practice of traditional Chinese medicine (TCM). The World Health Organization officially recognizes TCM as a form of complementary and alternative medicine, and the practice is taught side by side with Western biomedicine in many Chinese teaching hospitals and medical schools. Thus, the use of "traditional medicine" to describe non-Western systems has quickly become a mainstay in global health discourse. While many works of medical anthropology also employ the term, a critical sensibility also exists around use of the term "traditional" involving what scholars call its Orientalist implications (Said 1978).

As I quickly found in my research, words and classifications impose restricting, if not obfuscating, borders—along with Orientalist or "othering" implications. By Orientalist, I mean that use of the term "traditional" in particular can imply a sort of timeless state, with traditions seen as static relics. We tend to derive a sense of nostalgia from their dependability. As it draws on romanticized notions of the old and rooted, "tradition" juxtaposes to "modernity." While many of the remedies in Kuwdé have existed for centuries, new medicines also constantly emerge in response to both physical and social demands. I aim to avoid such binaries (old versus new, traditional versus modern), searching for terminology that encapsulates traits of modernity within long-embedded practice. While I am aware that it is no panacea, I prefer the term "local" to "traditional" or "indigenous" medicine. This language will gain greater relevance when I speak of encounters between biomedicine and Kabre medicine. To think through the social and relational nature of medicine—expanding the notion of a medical system's *work*—a particular aspect of local Kabre medicine will serve as a prime example. I refer to this as the House Medical System (HMS), a term derived from the Kabre language itself.

Entering the Conversation: A Quick Overview of Some Medical Anthropology Literature

The medical systems of non-Western cultures caught the eye of anthropologists early on and generated some brilliant, though intensely local, ethnographies. In these studies, Andrew Strathern notes, "Anthropologists tended to describe small-scale, isolated cultures as independent units without systematically setting these into a broader historical context" (Strathern and Stewart 1999: 213). Taken as insulated and relatively static, these systems were analyzed through the lens of the symbolic and the structural. Thus, the French anthropologist Claude Lévi-Strauss (1963, 1967) drew attention to the role of symbols in crafting healing systems of local significance and belief. And the British anthropologist E. E. Evans-Pritchard's theories of witchcraft heightened awareness of social and relational explanations for the misfortunes of disease and illness (Evans-Pritchard 1937).

As local medical systems entered into conversation with biomedicine, new comparisons, theoretical orientations, and methods of evaluation emerged. Along with them came challenges of resisting the currents of Orientalizing binaries. Early medical ethnographies often cast local medical systems as "fashionable" yet distinctly "other" subjects; "social development literature of the past" posited indigenous healing as contrapuntal to Western biomedicine (Kleinman 1984: 139; Singer 1989: 1199). Within this paradigm, biomedicine enjoyed—and in many circles continues to enjoy—a "critical immunity," shielded from critique by the assumed scientific impenetrability of Western practice. This ideology yielded both medical and social science research that translated "devils into parasites . . . jealousies as a way of talking about social inequalities . . . angry ancestors as disturbances in the psyche" (Langwick 2011: 8). Stacey Langwick's observation highlights the overwhelming tendency to slot local and traditional accounts into Western biomedical categories. Yet the politics of such translation also shielded traditional medicine from its own autonomy, limiting the extent to which local practice could work *independently of* biomedicine.

Margaret Lock credits the medical anthropologist Allan Young with inspiring a shift toward envisioning local medical systems as symmetrical to biomedicine. In his writings during the 1980s, Young emphasized the need to consider medical systems as knowledge practices produced by their social, historical, and political contexts. With this "understanding of how medical facts are predetermined by the processes through which they are . . . produced," the task of comparative medical anthropologies became to "critically examine the *social conditions* of knowledge production" (Lock and Nguyen 2010: 59; emphasis added). Such symmetry of analysis freed the study of local medical systems, which were no longer defined solely by their contrast with biomedicine. Just as biomedical knowledge emerged from a long history of Western thought, local medical systems could provide insight to their cognitive and social origins.

A recent focus within medical anthropology on the concept of embodiment seeks to place the body at the center, studying what Nancy Scheper-Hughes (1994: 230) calls "medicine's *regard*—its focused and sustained gaze on (or inside) the body." Following Arthur Kleinman's identification of multiply layered and locally constructed understandings of sickness, disease, and illness, Scheper-Hughes defines not one but three "bodies" of interest: "the representational *body social*; the controlling, bio-power forces of the *body politic*; and . . . attribution of meanings to the individual and existential *body personal*" (Scheper-Hughes 1994: 231). This multivalent analysis of the body provides a useful optic in contrast to the singular "Universal Body" of biomedicine.

Paramount among cross-cultural studies of medical systems is the question of efficacy (Kirmayer 2004; Nichter 1992; Waldram 2000). This issue tends to problematically adhere to a narrow conception of what is "efficacious" and what is not, whereas in reality "what counts as a good outcome may range from change in a discrete behaviour . . . or improved 'quality of life' to the restoration of harmony between body, social order, and the cosmos" (Kirmayer 2004: 42). A refocusing of ethnomedical study from strictly conceived "efficacy" to situated "meaning" allows anthropologists to probe at the multiple ways a system can heal—physically, socially, spiritually, and relationally. According to Kirmayer, the allure of healing systems—biomedical *and* local—derives primarily from their operation within a larger set of cultural ideologies, values, and meanings (Kirmayer 2004: 43). My position is that we can better explain efficacy by thinking embodiment and power relations together, at the local and global levels. Like James Waldram (2000), I argue for a more fluid, open-ended conception of efficacy that allows for multiple notions of "meaning."

The debate here within the study of local medical systems is endemic to anthropology on a larger scale: how can one reconcile the individual (body) and the local and global contexts (cultures) in which it exists? Furthermore, how do these lenses, dually, construct notions of health, social identity, and the body? And perhaps most relevant, how do we evaluate the efficacy of systems operating on paradigms far different from those of biomedicine? To answer, or at least address, these questions requires an integrated consideration of embodiment, symbolism, and etiology alongside power, exchange, and the maintenance of sociopolitical order. Here, the Kabre HMS enters.

Kabre Ethnoanatomy: Beyond the Clinical Gaze

At their core, medical/healing systems address and treat the body. This lends the illusion of simplicity. But the immense diversity of medical systems indicates vast variability in the meaning, understanding, and visceral experience of the "body."[3] The house medical system local to Kuwdé emerged in response to, and as a product of, a uniquely Kabre philosophy of the body, its boundaries, and its susceptibility to disease. Thus, examining the work of Kabre medicine necessitates identifying what bodies—and illnesses—it emerged to work *on*. Claiming to decipher a culture's understanding of the body is an immense undertaking, which I cannot fully engage here. This section briefly and partially introduces the ways in which the Kabre conceptualize the body. An expansion of the paradigm for health beyond strictly Western biological definitions of the body better equips us to explore the types of work performed by the house medical system within Kabre culture.

Richard Alan Swanson (1985: 29) wrote,

> I, for instance, have never had the opportunity to see a real gene under an electron microscope. And even should I have had the opportunity I would be placing a certain degree of faith in the power of the microscope in showing me something I could not in fact see with my own unaided eyes. My faith in the existence of genes, however, is no less important or real than certain perceptions . . . about the human body.

His remarks remind us of the power of the lens for both medicine and anthropology. The lens of the electron microscope enables us to see and envision cellular and molecular forces at work that are invisible to the naked eye and far from the reaches of the human imagination. Likewise, the lens provided to us by our culturally crafted conceptions of our surroundings and ourselves influences how we see and experience our physicality. To assess the efficacy of medical systems in treating the "body," we must first identify—and gaze through—the particular lens through which that body sees and lives.

In biomedicine, we often think of the body proper as a physical container of a more amorphous and abstract self. Scheper-Hughes describes the "clinical gaze" of biomedicine: "Whereas biomedicine presupposes a universal, ahistorical subject, medical anthropologists are confronted with . . . bodies that refuse to conform (or submit) to presumably universal categories and concepts of disease, distress, and medical efficacy" (Scheper-Hughes 1994: 239). A culture's conceptualization of the body and its borders thus produces differential experiences. The body becomes a stage of sorts on which these relationships are negotiated. But the body is not just a stage; it is also an actor negotiating these relationships, for as Scheper-Hughes emphasizes, "Sickness is more than just an unfortunate brush with nature . . . more than something that 'just happens' to people. Sickness is something that humans do in uniquely original and creative ways" (Scheper-Hughes 1994: 232). In this section, I employ an expanded appreciation for the ways in which the body is both acted on and acts—and how disease becomes not a passive experience but an active assertion of identity, relationality, and power.

In general terms, the Kabre body cohabits naturalistic, spiritual, and relational space. Although the Kabre concept of the body is, on one level, corporeal and physical, it also consists of invisible entities. My introduction to this philosophy of being occurred under a shaded structure in the courtyard of a Farendé homestead. This frond-sheathed refuge proved an ideal interview site, and on a sweltering mid-July afternoon the healer Jesper lead me through his description of the Kabre body. "The Kabre person is composed of four parts," Jesper explained, "the body, the soul, the star, and the warito." The physical body is the only part visible to the human eye. However, as Jesper noted, "alone, the body is useless; the body dies. . . . Death also results from a departure of the soul." The star refers to the belief that "every person is also a star in the universe," placing the body in a universal context. The warito, which will be examined subsequently in greater detail, refers to one's "shadow person."

Rather than compartmentalized into units or organs, the Kabre body is multiply extended. The Kabre notion of warito, in particular, epitomizes the unseen qualities inherent to the self. "Warito," which translates literally as "behind person" or "shadow person," is just that: a reflection of one's self; a double. "Each warito is unique; it is like DNA or a fingerprint," Jesper explained. At first, the significance of this analogy eluded me. It seemed a perfectly appropriate way to depict the "uniqueness" of the warito, but it was not until later that I realized that Jesper had used a distinctly biomedical concept, DNA, to illustrate a local philosophy. His cunning turn challenges the notion that the two occupy mutually exclusive spheres.

Jesper qualified the interrelation and interdependence among these four constituent parts: "The four are interconnected, always, elemental. A good relationship between them means health. You miss one, and you are sick, or dead. But some sicknesses strike only one [part]." For the warito, Jesper noted, "you have to know him or her, you meet him or her to find out what he or she wants." It follows, then, that the Kabre define health by a sound and intimate knowledge of one's warito. As a corollary, disease often indicates a lack of adherence to the warito. Kabre local medicine reflects this belief; in the case of illness, an individual must consult their warito to learn the appropriate steps to restore health. Often, a diviner, a healer with clairvoyant connection to the spirit world, must facilitate this consultation. Remedies incorporate these idiosyncrasies; the diviner heeds the needs of the warito by tweaking and individualizing treatment regimens.

These multiple understandings of the body as an individual entity and a system of entwined parts—material and spiritual—paint a complex picture. While all of Kabre body philosophy cannot be distilled into Jesper's categorizations, they do provide a sketch of the ways in which the Kabre body is seen as compartmentalized but also whole. The unseen components and qualities of the person are constantly invoked through sacrifice, divination, and communication with spirits and ancestors. Codependence between parts—"a good relationship between them"—yields equilibrium understood and experienced as health. Kabre healing "works" to knit together not only this bodily multiplicity, but also, as we will subsequently see, people and bodies relationally into a community.

Equilibrium among the individual's multiple constituents determines wellness for the Kabre. Relationships among and between people also influence health and disease. As Charles Piot (1999: 18) notes, "Persons here [in Kuwdé] do not 'have' relations; they 'are' relations." Many Kabre attribute social origins to explain disease—physical manifestations of failed or troubled relationships, indebtedness, and ill will—all of which affect the material body. Relationality, for the Kabre, manifests in three main arenas: interpersonal, with the spirits, and with the ancestors. By investigating the multiple dimensions of Kabre relationality, we see how the HMS addresses and distinguishes among them, a form of social work unto itself.

Kotong Susoko: A Case Study of the Body as a Social-Relational Subject

One can invite this malady.
—Pascal Kei, speaking about kotong susoko

One disease, referred to by the Kabre as kotong susoko (bigness disease), is understood in purely relational terms. The disease exhibits itself as gross swelling of limbs and appendages. Biomedically, the swelling may indicate kidney or liver failure, a possible form of hydropsy, according to François, a medical assistant at a local (biomedical) health clinic. But for the Kabre, kotong susoko has an intensely interpersonal causation. A scarlet letter of sorts, the swelling indicates a poisoned relationship among either friends or family. The physical manifestation—being grossly enlarged—serves as a source of social stigmatization, one the sufferer would be ashamed to bear. Although the village members I spoke with attributed the disease to various causes—for example, two families refusing to speak, a wife's refusal of her husband's sex, a husband's rejection of his wife's moto[4]—all scenarios involved disruption of social relations and Kabre gender roles. These disputes should not be confused with misunderstandings or lapses of judgment. According to the local healer Pascal Kei, kotong susoko results from "*willfully* resisting good social conduct—when you know better, but choose to act otherwise."

As Piot explains, relationships among the Kabre are based on hierarchies of exchange and debt (Piot 1993: 362). Contrary to early Africanist schools of thought that painted romanticized images of egalitarian ethnic groups, hierarchy is actually actively sought and maintained. Disease narratives remind individuals of their roles within this hierarchy; physical swelling indicates deviation and imbalance among these relationships. Furthermore, and unlike many diseases that seem to operate "invisibly" within the body, swelling is extremely visible, hyper-present, and noticeable even with the most fleeting of glances. It makes sense, then, that such a publicly visible malady should be linked to exposing publicly relevant rejections of social mores.

The transitive nature of physical symptoms—past those directly involved and into those proximally related—indicates the social vulnerability of the body, bearing the physical repercussions of another's actions. That is, social consequences for the dishonesty of one can span beyond the body of the individual, harming another. The fact that kotong susoko can strike a child of an offending individual furthers the extent to which the disease threatens a sense of Kabre reproduction and lifecycle. Revolt against the family, a husband's refusal of his wife's moto or sex, or rejection of amity among fellow Kabre unravels the social threads of the village. The risk of disease and bodily vulnerability thus leverages a warning against these social and relational transgressions.

Once the physical sickness of kotong susoko has been incited, one cannot avoid it unless the aggressor admits to wrongdoing. Prevention of the malady requires timely repentance and pardon. Confession and reparation of relationships enables health, saving the body from this "very grave disease." If repentance is performed in time, as several healers told me, one can even avoid the physical effects of the disease altogether. Confession as a therapeutic tool is not unique to Kabre medical epistemology; the practice is widely employed even in biomedical environments as a means of empowerment and a symbolic step in the healing process. In the case of the HIV/AIDS epidemic across Africa, international human rights groups during the late 1990s worked to encourage people living with HIV to "come out" about their condition. This confession of illness produced social vulnerabilities—chastising remarks, stigmatization, blame, even violence and familial estrangement. Yet with time, the process became equated with a "first step" toward empowering health-seeking behavior (Lock and Nguyen 2010: 298). Thus, making public the intimacies and struggles of one's body is said to catalyze healing in many medical cultures.

Ancestry and the Body

Much as the spirit world tempers and mediates the Kabre body, the ancestral world influences the equilibrium. Ancestors, for the Kabre, are family members who have passed away. Unlike the spirits, ancestors are believed to inhabit the homestead long after their passing, living alongside their progeny. Although they are not physically present, their existence continues through relationships to the living. Many, if not all, house medicine remedies find their roots in ancestral knowledge, passed on through generations. Sacrifices and payments to the ancestors, described later, thank ancestors for protecting and guarding the health of the individual. Forgetting to deliver due gratitude—or perhaps more grave, doing so incorrectly— could incite further illness. Indeed, this issue became apparent in my fieldwork process. During a discussion with a work group shortly after I arrived,[5] I announced my interest in learning about local remedies in Kuwdé. One worker replied, "We want to show you our herbs, but in order to do this, we must first ask permission from the ancestors. If you take an herb when someone isn't sick, someone will get sick." His remark indicated a sense of indebtedness and vulnerability of an individual's health at the hands of the ancestors. Caring for one's body implicitly involves caring for and respecting one's antecedents; the two worlds are thus interlinked.

The House Medical System as Relational Practice

On a walking tour of his fields, Kérékou, a healer and local chief of a cluster of homesteads in Kuwdé, noted, "Three things grow in our fields: crops, trees, and medicines." He added with emphasis, "We do not cultivate medicine." It may come as a surprise that, in a community of some of the most

2.1 Kérékou, holding one of the many wild plants Kabre use as medicine.

2.2 Kérékou holds another local medicine. Kabre use all parts of the plant—leaves, roots, and seeds—in their medicine, each with its own specific healing properties.

skilled and able-bodied cultivators in Togo, remedies, unlike crops, are not grown for subsistence. These wild plants are also distinguished from weeds, which the Kabre meticulously remove by hand from their fields. The land, in essence, is a verdant pharmacopeia.[6] That medicines grow uncontained and wild is a symbol of their potency, especially in a community of cultivators.

Just as the Kabre orient to the land as a garden of medicines, they are similarly oriented to which houses in the village cure which ills. Ask any member of Kuwdé which house medicines belong to which houses, and with little hesitation they will generate a list. For instance, members will say, "If you have swollen glands or difficulty swallowing, you must visit the house of Sandi for his medicine; if you are struck by la maladie rouge [a skin rash] you go to the house of Pikam; if you have come into contact with a corpse, you go to Kouwènam's." Familiarity with the location and distribution of certain remedies within Kuwdé seems as naturalized as the network of paths connecting homesteads.

The HMS is structurally and functionally organized based on Kabre principles of relationality and complementarity so that it performs social-relational work at the regional, village, and family levels. The act of health seeking within this system orients the health seeker to his or her relative place within the village, the family, and the ancestral lineage. This social orientation forms the identity of a patient's body within the context of village community. Furthermore, the delegation and passing on of medicines also requires Kabre to actively negotiate their relationships and comportment within the family. Embedded within, remedy payment practices illustrate a negotiation of relationships not only with the healer (who provides the medicine) but also with the ancestors, from whom the knowledge of the remedy originates. Thus, falling ill is not an anomaly experienced by bodies in isolation but an experience that is tightly interwoven with social life. By seeking a return to health, the Kabre person must navigate and negotiate relationships both with his or her own body and with other Kabre.

HMS: Mapping Relationally Organized Medicine

The specific pairing of house with medicine is not arbitrary but precisely articulated, with emphasis on complementarity between parts. Fundamentally, this distribution follows the clan and gender hierarchies of Kuwdé.

Village and House Hierarchies

When I asked my subjects to recount a list of house medicine distributions among the village, I was repeatedly struck by how a certain few remedies and houses always came first. The remedies for grave illnesses (such as infertility, kotong susoko, or snakebite) are assigned to more ceremonially significant houses. This purposeful and articulate assignment reflects and reproduces village hierarchy. Although access to the treatment system may be available to all, specific knowledge of how to invoke and apply a treatment remains intensely secret, the property of its particular homestead. While the relative significance of homesteads within Kuwdé indeed depends on forces outside health and medicine (such as ancestral histories), the HMS continually produces and reiterates relationships of hierarchy and complementarity within the village.

Whereas the diviner-healers Hamidou and Kérékou said that their knowledge of remedies could be given to people outside the family, house

2.3 A woman walks the paths connecting homesteads and fields in the village of Kuwdé.

healers keep remedies strictly within the family. Such domaining gestures to Kabre deference to houses and families as entities. As Kouwènam explained, "The family *owns* the medicine, and one person within the family has the right to treat with it." An HMS medicine will not work correctly if, for instance, someone outside of the house tries to treat someone with it. Attempting to do so could have disastrous consequences; according to Henri, "It can create spiritual . . . even physical . . . side effects." Fear of such side effects and consequences presumably keeps remedies within the domain of their house. Furthermore, each healer I spoke with echoed one central feature of the HMS: "The father passes the remedy to his son."[7] As Jesper explained, "The child who receives the medical knowledge is *chosen*. He is normally the most curious child in the house, but also the most respectful." Jesper emphasized respect when asked how the child inheritor is selected. Respect for the healer role reinforces the importance of reverence to one's father/ancestor, rewarding the good behavior of progeny.

While intensely hierarchical in many respects, the diffuse distribution of medicines among houses in Kuwdé also operates on principles of complementarity. The very fact that medicines are distributed in the first place, rather than concentrated in one or two key homesteads, is telling.

As Kouwènam informed me, "Each house carries, at most, two to three house medicines." This principle harks to the notion of health as the business of the village; the whole (village) is necessary to heal the part (an individual's body). Furthermore, treating the *entire* body relies on a concerted effort from multiple houses that make up the village.

Gendered Relations

The village of Kuwdé is divided into two gendered clans—the male and the female. Male and female, in this context, do *not* refer to sexual gender; both clans consist of male *and* female members.[8] Rather, this division is a cultural one tied to ancestral and spiritual histories and provides a division of labor for ritual activity. By virtue of their attachment with specific houses, diseases and medicines themselves also get assigned positions within the Kabre gendered clan system. Two remedies in particular reinforce the gendered identity of their homestead within the village: the treatments for infertility and snakebite, which rest in key houses of the female and male clans, respectively.

Infertility

Perhaps the gravest of bodily ills within Kabre culture is the inability to conceive and produce a child. The production of life vitally perpetuates the house and clan. Couples that are unable to birth a child are considered ill with *kokode kotong* (disease of the womb). They seek to reverse their infertility by visiting the homestead of Pokare, one of the top-ranking houses in the female clan. According to the healer Pokare, kokode kotong strikes a couple, not solely the husband or the wife. This dualistic notion of disease sharing as a product between two people—not unlike offspring—is inherently reflected in the HMS treatment itself. As Pokare recounted: "The woman comes in the middle of the night to get the medication. The medicine has two parts. She drinks the first medicine. Then, she covers her skin with the second. The naked woman covers herself with a cloth and stands over an open fire. The fire, along with the medication, goes into her body. The next day, she and her husband drink the first medication again. If the treatment does not work, the couple is truly infertile. Or, the warito may accept or refuse treatment."

The remedy itself is ripe with reproductive symbolism. By standing over the fire, she allows the medicine to enter "into her body," a form of symbolic insemination. If after visiting Pokare the woman regains her fertility and successfully gives birth, Pokare, rather than the woman's husband, is considered the "father" of the children; the children themselves refer to him as "father." Such a practice invokes the extended philosophy of person and body. Births, like bodies, are relational phenomena rather than strictly biological. Half-jokingly but also seriously, Pokare remarked about the fact that he had "so many . . . hundreds of children" throughout Kuwdé, Farendé, and other surrounding villages. Read in the context of the medicine's delivery ritual, it is as if Pokare himself, or as a vessel of the gendered power of his house, inseminates the woman. By restoring her capacity for childbirth, he is dually restoring her ability to become a productive member of Kuwdé, actively populating the village. Reference to Pokare as "father" hails, in an Althusserian sense, not only the medicine, but also the house itself, affirming its potency in the female clan.

Pokare's account provides its own reference to work ("If the treatment does not *work*, the couple is truly infertile"). Yet "work" here is defined by its antonym: the continuation of the illness (infertility). By "working," Pokare's remedy is restoring gender to the bodies of both the man and the woman: their ability to produce offspring. Why is it necessary for gender identities to be reinforced by Pokare's treatment? And why is such careful attention paid to the performance of the remedy? According to Piot, there is a "power and efficacy" to Kabre public ritual, so that "through ritual, identities and relationships are made known, 'visible,' and thus real, to others" (Piot 1999: 77). Gender, for the Kabre, is repeatedly performed and asserted; its biological evidence alone does not suffice. Remedies within the HMS, such as Pokare's infertility medicine, act on bodies that must assert their gender through activity. The very act of taking an HMS medicine mirrors and facilitates such an assertion.

Snakebite

The house of Sam, head of the male clan, holds knowledge of the treatment for snakebite. Although this was not explicitly stated by those with whom I spoke, one could infer that the entrusting of the snakebite remedy to Sam's house was not a coincidence. In addition to the phallic symbolism of snakes in Kabre society, more men than women are bit by snakes because men cultivate the fields (where snakes hide). Thus, it follows that the power of the male clan must be invoked to expel poison and heal. The ceremonial payment structure, in which the victim of snakebite gives thanks for the medicine, also invokes gendered performance. Sam outlined a facet of this payment: "You must cut the outside toe of a female chicken, take the blood, and put it on the foyer where the woman cooks. If the bitten person is truly good, the chicken will live a long life and give many eggs." The invocation of the female—the female chicken, the blood, the act of cooking, and the production of eggs—is itself rich with symbols of fertility. By performing this rite, the snakebite victim makes public the restoration of wellness and return to production.

In addition to successfully expelling the venom and healing the bite, the remedy has a second effect, as Sam described: "The snake [that bit you] will die if you place the medicine on the bite." This added dimension exemplifies the symbolic power of the healing ritual. Indeed, the snake's death is more symbolically understood than physically enacted. More often than not the snake's physical carcass is not recovered, and the snake is assumed to have died in the bush. This requires a dimension of belief in the healing process; a Kabre entrusts a certain measure of belief in the power of the male clan—and Sam's remedy—to affect something he may not visibly "see." By seeking restoration of health from Sam's house, the victim dually endorses and vests his belief in the potency of the male clan to heal snakebite. Indeed, belief is an integral element of the social. This facet of Sam's remedy reiterates that health and illness, for the Kabre, occur between—rather than just within—people and bodies.

Other Gendered Remedies

While the remedies for infertility and snakebite exemplify the gendered allocation of medicines to Kabre homesteads, the gendered placement of house medicines extends further. In addition to infertility, Pokare's house treats a serious malady that strikes children, characterized by episodes of seizing and referred to as *sumura kotong* (bird disease). As child-rearing in Kuwdé primarily falls within the domain of the mother, or related women, it seems logical that the remedy would reside in a female clan house.

The homestead of Kouwènam, another important house within the female clan, owns the remedy *hilum kori* (wind medicine). According to Kouwènam, hilum kori treats a Kabre illness that strikes those who take care of the sick: "The wind carries the stench of the ill person's body, and you cannot hold your stomach. You cannot eat well; you have no appetite, you have intestinal discomfort, indigestion, vomiting, and nausea. This remedy gives you back your appetite." Again, women are entrusted with the role of caring for cadavers, or dying bodies. Like sumura kori, hilum kori calls on those who are implicated in caregiving—women—and thus must reside only in a female clan house.

In the process of seeking remedies, the Kabre are implicitly interpellated within the gendered organization of the village. In this sense, the HMS works to reflect and echo house identity within the gendered clan system. Furthermore, the remedies themselves directly (and more materially) invoke the sick person's body in a way that enacts and defines gender.

Spoken and Unspoken: A Return to "Work"

Often, anthropology and theory fall subject to the very same skepticism that traditional medicine encounters: "What *work* do they do?" What is the value of immaterial critique? What does it solve? Anthropologists, and the discipline of anthropology itself, must grapple with this self-consciousness and self-awareness. I, too, grappled with it, as a student of anthropology and throughout the course of this research. One question posed throughout this project haunted me for months: "So *what*?" This question was emblematic of more questions and doubts that circulated through the fieldwork and writing process. What were the larger implications of my work to the grounded realities and complexities of health, tradition, and modernity in modern Togo?

This vein of questioning exposes a parallel and concomitant project: understanding, affirming, and recharting the role of anthropology in global health and the "work" it can perform. In arenas of policy making and other applied contexts, anthropology offers resonant contributions that beg examination. While often criticized as esoteric or obtuse, the language and words we speak reveal (and create) our world and our space. Just as the politics of translation complicate the interpretation of Kabre into French, and French into English, the translation between medical epistemologies trafficks in power and politics. The rhetoric of medical pluralism, often lauded and praised, serves an important arena to probe and push. Much of the current literature asserting the role of anthropology in global health practices still perpetuates this notion of co-optation, more heavily weighted toward forwarding health policy goals. While these concrete goals (reducing maternal mortality rates, improving public hygiene, increasing access to biomedicine) are noble in their own right, they often obfuscate local experiences, offering only a partial, Westernized "health."

A central role of anthropology thus surfaces: bringing awareness to what gets spoken *and* what goes unspoken. People in Kuwdé live their medical system, each and every day. There is a lot that we live that we may never articulate; this does not mean it does not exist. The role of anthropology is thus to acknowledge that which silently and invisibly moves. This acknowledgment, in turn, can expand notions of work and efficacy to encapsulate a broader conception of health and body. Doing so, I argue, enables a more complete healing—in its multiple dimensions.

Notes

1. *Alafia* is also a Yoruba word that likely has Hausa and Arabic roots.
2. Proving the physiological efficacy of Kabre medicines is beyond the purview of my research and knowledge and thus falls outside the scope of this essay. However, I caution against the desire to "prove" the physiological work of Kabre medicine in curing disease. Because this herbal system has been around for hundreds of years, and because people in northern Togo do overcome disease and illness to live long lives, we can assume it is also physiologically efficacious.
3. The term "ethnoanatomy" is borrowed from Richard Swanson and refers to how the anatomy of the human body is culturally constructed (Swanson 1985: 30).
4. *Moto*, a sorghum or cornmeal porridge, is a staple of the Kabre diet during the rainy season. Here, rejection of *moto* is also read as the refusal of a wife's sex, as symbolic correlation exists between fertility and women's food production in Kuwdé (Piot 1999).
5. A *haja*, or group of male cultivators.
6. Yet the herbs invoked in HMS treatments are not all available in the immediate vicinity of the village. As in the case of Tikénawe, many specialists and their families travel long distances to procure certain plants that are specific to a remedy.
7. Some remedies are passed to female members of the homestead; this occurs at the father's discretion. Indeed, Tikénawe learned several medicines from her father, which she currently uses.
8. Gender for the Kabre is a performed, rather than a naturalized, category.

References

Evans-Pritchard, E. E. 1937. *Witchcraft, Oracles, and Magic among the Azande*. Oxford: Clarendon.

Kirmayer, Laurence J. 2004. "The Cultural Diversity of Healing: Meaning, Metaphor, and Mechanism." *British Medical Bulletin* 69: 33–48.

Kleinman, Arthur. 1984. "Indigenous Systems of Healing: Questions for Professional, Popular, and Folk Care." In *Alternative Medicines*, ed. J. W. Salmon, 138–64. London: Tavistock.

Langwick, Stacey. 2011. *Bodies, Politics, and African Healing: The Matter of Maladies in Tanzania*. Bloomington: Indiana University Press.

Lock, Margaret, and Vinh-Kim Nguyen. 2010. *An Anthropology of Medicine*. West Sussex, UK: Wiley-Blackwell.

Nichter, Mark. 1992. "Ethnomedicine: Diverse Trends, Common Linkages." In *Anthropological Approaches to the Study of Ethnomedicine*, ed. Mark Nichter. Amsterdam: Gordon and Breach Science.

Piot, Charles. 1993. "Secrecy, Ambiguity, and the Everyday in Kabre Culture." *American Anthropologist* 95, no. 2: 353–70.

———. 1999. *Remotely Global: Village Modernity in West Africa*. Chicago: University of Chicago Press.

Said, Edward W. 1978. *Orientalism*. New York: Vintage.

Scheper-Hughes, Nancy. 1994. "Embodied Knowledge: Thinking with the Body in Critical Medical Anthropology." In *Assessing Cultural Anthropology*, ed. Robert Borofsky, 229–40. New York: McGraw-Hill.

Singer, Merrill. 1989. "The Coming of Age of Critical Medical Anthropology." *Social Science and Medicine* 28, no. 11: 1193–203.

Strathern, Andrew, and Pamela J. Stewart. 1999. *Culture and Healing: Medical Anthropology in Global Perspective*. Durham, NC: Carolina Academic Press.

Swanson, Richard Alan. 1985. *Gourmantché Ethnoanthropology*. Lanham, MD: University Press of America.

Waldram, James B. 2000. "The Efficacy of Traditional Medicine: Current Theoretical and Methodological Issues." *Medical Anthropology Quarterly* 14, no. 4: 603–25.

3. Biomedicine and Traditional Healing
Is Collaboration Possible?
Stephanie Rotolo

My research posed the following related questions: What are the implications of traditional healing and biomedicine coexisting in the same space? How might collaboration be fostered between them? I spent two months in northern Togo interviewing healers, diviners, and medical personnel at local clinics, as well as a range of villagers, to better understand the complexity of health care within the community. I found that despite the recent emergence of biomedicine in the villages, business within the traditional system has continued with vigor. In fact, patients commute between the different systems, seeking treatment from both. The point was brought home to me one day when I was interviewing an elderly herbalist about his remedy for an ear infection. After fifteen minutes, his wife emerged from a room in the homestead with an X-ray in hand. The old man then told me the story of an illness he had been trying to treat for three years. When treatment from one of the village's healers failed to work, he sought care from a hospital several miles away. Without enough money for further treatment at the hospital, the man returned home with his X-ray; his only option left was to get medicine from the local clinic that would suppress his symptoms for a few days at a time. This intermingling of modern technology and biomedicine with "traditional" herbal remedies turned out to be a common occurrence. We in the United States are inclined to separate "modernity" from "tradition"—in this case, the biomedical from indigenous medicines—imagining that once someone goes over, he or she does not come back. My research showed that such neat and mutually exclusive categorizations do not apply in Togolese villages (and probably much of the world). No one system has dominance over the other. Rather, traditional healing and biomedical practices complement each other, filling in gaps where each system reaches its limits (of remedy and explanation).

I begin this chapter by briefly surveying some of the literature on medical pluralism, followed by a description of my methods of data collection. I then explore how the seemingly distinct paradigms of biomedicine and traditional healing interact with each other in the villages of northern Togo and conclude with a call for collaboration to deliver appropriate medical care more effectively and efficiently within these medically pluralist communities.

Literature Review

As mentioned earlier, Togo practices a pluralist system of health-care provision that draws simultaneously on the paradigms of biomedicine and local or traditional healing. Literature on medical pluralism suggests that these paradigms are often seen by Euro-American and local biomedical practitioners as at odds and opposed to each other (Green 2008). Traditional medicine is considered static and inward-looking, not open to innovation or progressive modification (Yangni-Angaté 2000). It is also regarded as less effective. Modern biomedicine, by contrast, is thought to be progressive and forward-looking and is constantly undergoing innovation and advances through new research (Yangni-Angaté 2000). The use of the terms "traditional" and "indigenous" is part of the problem. When "traditional" is evoked as the opposite of "modern" or "scientific," it reproduces a divide that easily slips into hierarchized notions of tradition and modernity (or, earlier, of primitive and civilized) (Green 2008).

Despite such Euro-American distinctions, many peoples in the world today—perhaps especially in sub-Saharan Africa—muddy the waters between the two, mixing and matching as they see fit and seeing little distinction between modernity and tradition. For local populations, combining what we see as two distinct systems makes pragmatic and economic sense. They are just trying to get by, to find the means to make themselves and their children healthy. But this is no longer just a case of local practice. National governments and international organizations such as the World Bank are now promoting the use of so-called traditional healing and the blending of the two systems (Langwick 2008). This is so not only because traditional medicines are cheaper and their use saves people (and governments) money but also because they are effective and widely used. In places such as Togo, for example, the number of traditional healers far exceeds that of modern doctors. All the while, their services remain largely unrecognized—and continue to be discriminated against—by the formal health sector (Serbulea 2005).

My work challenges attempts to keep the two modes of healing conceptually and practically separate and suggests that we need increasing collaboration between the two. Such collaboration makes cultural, economic, and health sense (Langwick 2008; Serbulea 2005). However, any such collaboration begs the following questions: What type of relationship between traditional healing and biomedicine is most appropriate for a particular ethno-locale? What are the benefits and drawbacks of collaboration? Can this community realistically support a unified health system, and how does one go about promoting the idea (Yangni-Angaté 2000)?

Methods

Research for this study was conducted in the rural villages of Kuwdé and Farendé, located in the north of Togo. The Kabre people who inhabit this area are primarily subsistence farmers, who have little to no disposable income. They live in clusters of straw- and tin-roofed houses without electricity or running water. Sanitation is poor, which creates an optimal breeding ground for water- and vector-borne diseases, particularly during the seven-month rainy season. According to the community's trained medical assistant, the villages are hardest hit by malaria, respiratory infections, and digestive and parasitic diseases. Decentralization of the state's money and power—since the 1990s—means that the villages rely heavily on donor aid and local resources for health services.

3.1 Kabre Homestead.

I carried out research in these two villages by conducting semi-structured interviews with local residents and supplemented these with informal conversations and observations. I spent mornings in discussion at the local health clinics, the Case de Santé (Health Hut) in Kuwdé and the Centre Médico-Sociale (CMS) in Farendé, and afternoons in the homesteads of healers, diviners, and the heads of those families that have house remedies (see Middleton, this volume).

Interviews and Observations at the Clinics in Kuwdé and Farendé

I interviewed medical assistants in their professional settings and asked them to describe diagnosis and treatment methodologies of the most common diseases in the villages. I posed additional interview questions to better understand how patients move between health-care systems and the resources the clinic can provide to patients that the traditional system lacks. I observed interactions between the medical assistants and patients during consultations, paying particular attention to descriptions of symptoms and accounts of previous treatment for illness.

I conducted fourteen interviews with those who specialize in house medicines in Kuwdé—in this community, the most important medicines are divided among houses (Middleton, this volume)—in addition to a smaller selection of recognized healers and diviners. Just as I did with the medical assistants, I asked these people to describe their specialties and how they go about diagnosing and treating patients. I also explored more generally how they conceptualize disease. Finally, I asked all about their relationship to and experiences with the local biomedical clinics.

Informal Conversations with Villagers

I often engaged in less formal discussions with villagers during non-work hours and at community gatherings.[1] People readily voiced their opinions about how they respond to illness, beginning with the recognition of symptoms and continuing through the healing process. They spoke openly about the differences between clinicians and healers, and between pharmaceuticals and herbal medicines.

The Anatomy of a "Traditional" Medical System

"In Africa, all diseases have two faces: natural and spiritual," claimed François, the one trained medical assistant in the village of Farendé. To become a medical assistant, one must pass the baccalaureate exam at the end of high school, then successfully complete an admissions exam for medical school. A student studies there for three years, has to pass a battery of exams, and writes a thesis before being placed at a health center where she or he is authorized to treat patients.

While François practices only biomedicine in his clinic, he does not deny the rich culture and tradition of herbal medicine rooted in the surrounding communities, where despite the introduction of biomedicine more than fifty years ago, traditional healing remains a cornerstone of local practice. Traditional healing provides explanations for and solutions to physical, social, spiritual, and even political issues that arise in the community.

This local health-care system is extremely complex and intricate. Its main practitioners are healers who provide patients with herbal remedies for their illnesses, remedies learned from parents and grandparents. Those who dispense house medicines study their children and select the one or ones they trust in passing along knowledge. If the elders do not have children, they might turn to a nephew, thus keeping the knowledge in the family. Children often begin learning traditional remedies when they are young.

Individuals are taught all of the protocols associated with diagnosis and treatment, including dietary restrictions, dosage, and how to collect and store medicines. While men typically dominate this system, some women hold knowledge about medicines and treatment.

Importantly, given the stereotype many Euro-Americans and health professionals hold of traditional medicine as static and unchanging, as new diseases enter the community, healers experiment with new remedies to learn what might make patients better. They are constantly on the lookout for the new and the better. One healer, Jesper (who also served as my translator), told me, "When I go to new places and meet new people, I also attempt to learn about new remedies. Then I test them on myself to see if they really work before prescribing them for others." In this way, the community experiences constant innovation within its health-care practices.

Healers make diagnoses from observation and from their patients' descriptions of symptoms. Upon diagnosis, healers collect ingredients to cure the illness, with many medicinal plants gathered in the "bush" away from human habitation, even miles from a healer's homestead. Cultivating medicinal plants—as one would food such as corn, sorghum, or yams—is forbidden, and gathering them when someone is not sick will render treatment ineffective. Doing so, according to an elder I spoke to, might even make someone in the village fall ill.

Compensation for treatment is awarded when health is restored and typically comes in the form of local beer or a chicken. "If you go to a healer and he asks you for payment up front, he is a fake," Jesper warned. Once a patient is fully healed, he will return to the homestead where he originally sought treatment, bearing a chicken and homemade beer. The animal is sacrificed to the healer's ancestors and eaten by the healer alone. Similarly, the beer, which holds high social value within the community, is reserved for the healer to drink by himself. Both gifts also serve as recognition of the healer's ancestors, from whom knowledge of the treatment was handed down, and are vital to ensuring the efficacy of the medicine and maintaining order in the household. Occupying a critical community role, healers are respected leaders in the villages.

In addition to these healers, each house has its own remedies, with the heads of households acting as specialists for a particular disease. These community members form a part of a house system of remedies that are passed down through the generations (Middleton, this volume). Although the therapeutic process is quite similar to that practiced by the healers, medicinal knowledge within a household is limited to a single disease or set of diseases. Because the system is long-standing and remedies stay within a genealogy, knowledge of where to seek treatment for specific illnesses is shared by all community members—and everyone in the community has full access to, and is able to seek care from, any household.

Another type of specialist, a diviner, has the power of clairvoyance, which enables him to communicate with actors in the spiritual world. Unlike healers, diviners learn their powers and remedies directly from the spirits. Whereas healers treat illnesses of the body, diviners typically treat the underlying spiritual or social causes of disease. According to Kérékou, a healer and diviner, "Diviners can see witchcraft in action and have the power to stop it. They know how to communicate with the spirits." Unlike natural illnesses, spiritual maladies result from someone intentionally making you sick. Therefore, treatment is a question of diplomacy and psychology and must target the underlying social-spiritual causes. When a person falls ill and needs the assistance of a diviner to be restored to health, a friend or family member is sent in her or his place to speak with the diviner, as direct contact "may further complicate the affair." During such a visit, the diviner places cowry shells on divination stones to initiate a connection with the spirits. On behalf of the spirits, the diviner will ask the proxy family member or friend for specifics about the situation. Instruction for treatment is then communicated from the spiritual forces to the diviner, and from the diviner to the patient's proxy. Treatment may often combine herbal therapy with suggestions for behavioral change.

Severe illness of a spiritual nature occurs when an individual becomes disconnected from his double or "behind-person" (warito), a sort of shadow or soul. This might happen when a witch in the community is trying to do the person harm. The witch will give the person's double to an evil spirit, which will "eat" (kill) the victim if a diviner does not intercede. Thus, when someone becomes seriously ill, she or he will consult a diviner to discover whether the cause is witchcraft. If it is, the person might be asked to sacrifice an animal to undo the damage and coax her or his double back. If the person returns to health, she or he knows that the diviner's diagnosis was correct.

Indigenous medicine functions not only to heal physical maladies but also to return spiritual and social imbalances to equilibrium. Healers, house medicine specialists, and diviners take a holistic approach to health and sickness—a health holism that is deeply rooted in Kabre culture and its way of life and that stands in contrast to biomedicine.

Biomedicine as an Alternative Form of Healing

Biomedicine creates a rupture with traditional understandings of disease. The social, cultural, and symbolic aspects of disease do not factor into diagnosis and treatment; rather, biomedicine's focus is on the physical/biological body alone. Putatively grounded in natural facts and scientific evidence, biomedicine employs an entirely different framework and language for disease. Noting this distinction, Basile, a community health worker in Kuwdé, explained to me that he is unable to tell whether a disease is spiritually caused, but is responsible for treating the physical symptoms regardless.

The small clinic located in the center of the village of Kuwdé, the Case de Santé, was built primarily for birthing assistance, although it now treats a range of illnesses. It is staffed by two village health workers, originally nominated by their community to take on this role, who received two months of training when they began their practice in 1998. Since then, they have received intermittent training when donors and government officials visit to introduce new treatment regimens and programs.

At the Case de Santé, nearly all patient visits follow the same progression: patient describes symptoms; staff member measures vital signs; staff member prescribes medicine.[2] To every visit, patients bring her or his *carnet de santé*, a booklet in which people keep track of their medical history, thus allowing them to move among state- and NGO-sponsored clinics in different villages. Patients must pay money up front for the medicine they receive.

3.2 Kuwdé's Case de Santé.

In the neighboring village of Farendé, the CMS functions in much the same way as the Case de Santé. The CMS, however, is larger and has more resources and is thus able to respond to the health demands of a greater number of people. The staff has more specialized training, with the authority to use more advanced health technology (such as giving injections and using microscopes to detect malarial and other parasites). Despite their differences, the Case de Santé and CMS both assume the role of an alternative, biomedical approach to healing within their villages.

These local clinics operate at the mercy of the government and the donors who provide them with the resources they need to treat their patients and train their staff. Remedies are not found in the local environment, which means that practitioners cannot simply step into their backyards to gather appropriate treatment when the shelves in the clinic's pharmacy become empty. When the clinic's supply of diagnostic tests and antimalarial medicines runs out, for example, which it often does in the middle of the rainy season (when the incidence of malaria is high), the clinic has no choice but to improvise with the few resources it has or to send patients elsewhere for treatment. Without diagnostic tests, the clinic cannot differentiate between malaria and stomach worms, so it is assumed the patient has both and is then given individual drugs for each symptom. When the pool of money collected from payments for medicines runs out, the clinic is stuck waiting for the government or other donors to provide additional resources. Basile explained that the Case de Santé gets rapid diagnostic tests for malaria once a year, but he runs out of them quickly because malaria is the most prevalent disease in the area. Despite the high morbidity, the current donor-run supply system sets a limit on the number of diagnostic tests the clinic can receive each year. Because of the rarity of full restocks, patients are forced to turn to the local system or walk long distances to other clinics.

Although biomedical practitioners are far outnumbered by traditional healers, Basile claims that people go to the clinic because they feel they can get something there that the traditional system cannot provide.

The Biomedical in the Local

Despite assumptions to the contrary, Kabre indigenous medicine also has what border on biomedical understandings of disease. Germain, a local healer, offered an example that was highly dramatic because it came from what otherwise was the most spiritual of diseases in Kabre: *kotong susoko* (bigness disease). This rare but fatal disease, which is most closely translated as swollen extremities (hydropsy), is believed to be evidence of (caused by) the fact that the victim is her- or himself a witch. Neither the traditional nor the biomedical system within the villages has found a successful treatment for kotong susoko, with villagers consulting diviners to attend to the witchcraft and health clinicians providing medicine to treat kidney failure.

Despite the local view that kotong susoko is a disease with spiritual origins, however, the Kabre use methods to treat family and community members who have been in contact with a kotong susoko victim that are not unlike those of biomedicine. Germain described for me the ritual that occurs after someone with kotong susoko has died: a healer-diviner takes an herbal remedy to the house of the deceased to protect the rest of the family from the disease, lest its contagion allow it to continue to circulate through the village. As family members and friends enter the homestead, they rub the product on their chests and backs for protection. Once everyone is present in the courtyard, Germain adds another ground medicine to a calabash of local beer and passes it around for all to sip, further protecting themselves from the reemergence of the disease. Kai, the village chief, described the seriousness of this form of death. There is no dancing, as at most other funerals, and the body is not buried in one of the family tombs. The family burns all of the deceased's belongings and buries her or him in an isolated area away from all other tombs. The disease is brought by spirits, so a serious ritual is vital in pardoning the deceased's wrongdoing and preventing the disease from living on in the family. Note that despite its social-spiritual causes, the response to kotong susoko—of controlling the spread of physical contagion—overlaps with what we might expect of biomedicine.

In the rural villages, new biomedical tools and diagnostics are used alongside local traditions at increasing rates. Many healers have begun to incorporate, and sometimes even require, biomedical testing before distributing herbal medicines, which was never before a prerequisite to obtaining treatment. Jesper described an unusual instance of his own demand for proof before treatment. "Several years ago, an American Peace Corps Volunteer I knew got stomach worms and sought treatment from the U.S. Embassy doctor in Lomé," he said. "She was prescribed medicine but didn't want to take the drugs, preferring natural medicines. She came to me for help, and I asked to see the written diagnosis before treating her." He told another story about the hospital's inability to heal his cousin's broken bones: "My cousin broke his leg and spent three months in the hospital in Lomé. When his leg did not heal after all that time, he went to Ketao, where a healer asked him for his X-ray results before prescribing treatment."

At a meeting of some healers I attended, the chief of Farendé gave his blessing to this new phenomenon, explaining a new mandate within the state-recognized Association de Guérisseurs (Association of Healers) that requires patients to get biomedical analyses before receiving treatment from the traditional system. He described an instance in which he, a renowned healer in the village, felt the symptoms of malaria and went to the CMS to confirm his diagnosis. After receiving a positive rapid diagnostic test, he even purchased and treated himself with the clinic's prescribed pharmaceuticals rather than using his own herbal remedy. That is not to say that the villagers are shifting toward a new, more Euro-American biological outlook on health. Rather, the line between the local and the biomedical is blurring—or has always been blurred—and systems of understanding are slipping beyond their respective domains.

How Do People Make Use of Medical Pluralism?

Village conceptions and understandings of particular diseases as physical, natural, spiritual, or social often dictate where patients initially seek care. Many community members have opposing opinions of causation. Jesper, for example, asserted that all illnesses have spiritual causes. Every disease is sent from someone (an enemy, a witch) who is trying to make you sick. Tikenawé, a house specialist, refuted Jesper's claims by asking, "Why would someone [an enemy] send you a simple fever?" She added that each time she goes to Lomé, she gets sick, but she does not know anyone in the city who would send her illnesses. As the head of the Case de Santé and an advocate for its value within the village, Basile says that the origin of a disease should not always determine how it is treated. Not everyone goes to a diviner to find out who might be making her or him sick before getting treatment, and the fact that people go to the biomedical clinic (which does not treat the spiritual or social side of disease) further indicates that there are plural (and perhaps contested) conceptions of disease etiology within this small community.

Some people think that certain diseases can be treated by only one of the two systems, but that, too, is contested. For anemia, the Case de Santé and CMS clinicians assert that biomedicine is the only solution, whereas the healer Kérékou believes he can diagnose and treat patients with the same symptoms. "It is important that people come here first because healers cannot know for sure" whether someone has anemia, Basile says. In addition, he claims that "anemia cannot be treated quickly in the community" without drugs. Basile explained that the Case de Santé prescribes vitamins and hemoglobin and iron tablets to patients but also makes vital dietary recommendations that the traditional system fails to do. For rarer illnesses, the clinic's limited stock of essential medicines is unable to provide treatment. As a result, health-care providers may call on traditional healers to fill the gap. For example, the Case de Santé does not have appropriate products to treat high blood pressure. After providing behavioral suggestions, the Case de Santé typically sends patients back to healers for herbal remedies. François, the medical assistant at the CMS, even accepts that high blood pressure is a disease that is social-psychological in origin. However, biomedical diagnostics are important, health workers claim, because high blood pressure could be a sign of the presence of other diseases, including malaria. Similarly, what may appear to be a simple cough could be a serious case of tuberculosis.

François noted the importance of collaboration for chronic illnesses. Despite distinctions between the systems, resources are shared between healers and the clinics. This "sharing" is led predominantly by the patients, as they combine and use both sources of diagnosis and treatment in ways they find appropriate and beneficial to their health. Patients participate in a system of trial and error, as they admit that there is not necessarily a specific process to which they adhere in seeking treatment. As mentioned earlier, Jesper learns new remedies and tries them on himself before he prescribes them to anyone else. Tikenawé concurs: "When you get sick, you figure out how to get better." While she possesses the remedial knowledge of a few medicines passed down from her father, trial and error is what led her to be able to describe to me the treatments for eight simple illnesses she and her family have faced. Most of her knowledge comes from her own experiences with diabetes, high blood pressure, and anemia. For more serious conditions that she does not know well, Tikenawé says, she sends her family and friends to seek treatment from another house in the village or the clinic down the road.

If, after moving between biomedicine and the local system of healers and house specialists, neither system gives healing, people often turn to a diviner to see whether witchcraft is at the root of the problem. When seemingly natural causes in either system do not get fixed, and social adjustments and re-harmonization of social relations do not work, patients believe witchcraft is likely to be at play. With a naturalist conception of disease, Kouwènam, a villager, said people tend to test out several treatments, and if none works, they then seek advice from diviners. In particular, Jesper explained, people go to the hospital with symptoms seeking biomedical tests for confirmation. When Western medicine does not give answers, he said, they often accept that their diseases and treatment are out of human control. Tikenawé complicated this picture even more, saying, "When I first got sick, I went to the diviner, but that was too expensive. Now I go to the hospital, and if I do not respond to treatment, I leave it up to God. [She recently started attending a Christian church.]"

Emerging Demand for Collaboration

The fluidity between the two systems and the coexistence of remedies and biomedical analyses in a single home shows that many Kabre see these not as opposing entities but, rather, as facets of a larger pool of resources from which they can draw for their health-care needs. The discourse of collaboration, in addition to its evident material demonstration, notably has taken root in the villages. When asked whether traditional healing and biomedical practices should collaborate, most villagers, healers, and clinic staff responded positively, asserting that doing so brings the potential for improved health in the community.

Currently, the Association of Healers in the area is working to integrate the two systems and build recognition for healers within biomedical institutions. The association, on behalf of the wider community of healers, seeks to find a way for biomedicine to recognize traditional healing, and perhaps even consult it.

Originally created by Farendé's village chief, the association is made up of healers who are selected by reputation rather than through formal testing. During one of their meetings, participants spoke largely about the cross-referrals among healers and with the clinic. When faced with certain illnesses outside of his repertoire, one healer explained, he refuses to treat the patient and instead refers her or him to another healer who knows the treatment better, working within a system of reciprocity. Although compliance is low, an association policy also states that healers must send their patients to the biomedical clinic for analysis or diagnostics before providing treatment. This move toward professionalizing or normalizing traditional medicine is also apparent in the printout from the meeting, which referenced the Togolese Ministry of Health, putting the discourse of collaboration in the villages within a larger, statewide context.

As a culmination to my research, I co-organized a collaborative workshop that brought together healers and biomedical workers, many of whom I had spoken with during my stay. To ignite discussion and debate among the participants, I (and the other organizers) chose three illnesses for which both systems of treatment are often used (and over which difference of opinion exists about their cause and treatment)—malaria, high blood pressure, and kotong susoko—to serve as case studies. Participants filled the desks of the Farendé schoolhouse and spoke candidly about their

3.3 Healers' conference.

experiences providing and seeking care for these illnesses. While much consensus was reached on the necessity of collaboration, serious differences remained over the etiology and prescribed treatment for certain diseases. Many participants noted, however, that each system might play a complementary role in the diagnosis and treatment of these diseases. Farendé's village chief suggested sharing a list of healers and their products with the clinic and throughout the whole canton so that they may be called on when their services are needed. Others recommended involving healers in health training and hosting more regular discussions between healers and clinic staff. François asserted that the central question in moving the discourse of collaboration toward a practiced reality must be: what can modern medicine do that traditional healing cannot, and vice versa? This conversation struck me as a productive first step in furthering what will surely be the wave of the future: increased collaboration.

Conclusion

This essay does not argue for any formula or prescription—for a particular way forward in integrating traditional healing with biomedicine. Instead, it attempts to make the case that interactions between traditional healing and biomedicine already exist and are becoming increasingly prevalent in northern Togo and that dialogue between the two is already under way and constantly evolving in this postcolonial space—a point worth repeating in the face of a biomedical community and health professionals around the world who continue to see traditional medicine as less and other. The critical issue is how best to cultivate a relationship that plays to the strengths of each system to provide the most effective and efficient health care to the village community.

Notes

1. The term "villager" is not intended as condescending (as a contrast, for instance, to "city dweller"). Instead, I use the term to designate anyone in the villages other than recognized healers, diviners, and biomedical providers.
2. Invariably, pharmaceutical medicines are dispensed to treat a patient's symptoms. The medicines are sold for double their purchase price, thus generating income for the clinic.

References

Green, Lesley J. F. 2008. "'Indigenous Knowledge' and 'Science': Reframing the Debate on Knowledge Diversity." *Archaeologies* 4, no. 1: 144–63.

Langwick, Stacey A. 2008. "Articulate(d) Bodies: Traditional Medicine in a Tanzanian Hospital." *American Ethnologist* 35, no. 3: 428–39.

Serbulea, Mihaela. 2005. "Old Meets New in West Africa's Medicine Mix." SciDevNet. http://www.scidev.net/en/features/old-meets-new-in-west-africas-medicine-mix.html.

Yangni-Angaté, Antoine. 2000. "Traditional and Modern Medicine in the Context of Globalization." World Bank. https://openknowledge.worldbank.org/handle/10986/10769.

4. Rural Medicines in an Urban Setting
Kelly Andrejko

In Lomé, the bustling seaside capital of Togo, little has remained unchanged over the past century. From the ubiquitous motorcycle taxis to the streetside Akon music, Lomé is a city bursting at the seams with signs of the modern. Nevertheless, blending in among the gas stations and open-air markets is a long-standing system of healing: women on street corners with coolers of medicinal tea; market stands next to the vegetables selling up to a hundred different types of therapeutic leaves, roots, and bark. Despite the availability of biomedical care, everyone I spoke with in a cross-section of urban dwellers, from shop owners to doctors and civil servants, still relies on these herbal medicines. Everyone I interviewed still found use for herbal remedies, whether it was the occasional tisane (medicinal tea) at the end of an energy-draining day or a powder taken to cure infertility. In this essay, I explore the incidence of "traditional" medicine use in Lomé, asking who uses it and why, for which diseases, and at what point in the onset of illness. I was also interested in the movement of people between the biomedical and herbal systems. When do people stick to one system of care, and when do they shuffle between the two? In short, I explore the role village medicine continues to play in an urban context in West Africa.

Background

At the intersection of cultural anthropology and global health, an emerging area of interest is the role of traditional medicine within biomedicine. International health organizations, including the World Health Organization (WHO), recently have suggested that so-called traditional medicine be acknowledged as an important contributor to the health of populations. Herbal systems are often cheaper, more accessible, and just as effective as other, internationally endorsed treatments (WHO 2013). In fact, it is estimated that in some Asian and African countries, up to 80 percent of the population depends on traditional medicines as their primary form of health care, even though those medicines may not be legally recognized or regulated (Oreagba et al. 2011). This sale of non-pharmaceutical remedies also generates billions of dollars in revenue each year for local economies (Oreagba et al. 2011). Moreover, many pharmaceutical medications, including aspirin, digoxin, morphine, and quinine, are derived from plants and herbal remedies, with global health officials imagining that many more remain to be discovered (Vickers et al. 2001).

Despite the positive and potential contributions of "non-modern" medicine to the health of populations globally, many negative stereotypes remain. For many, the words "traditional medicine" evoke images of a medical practice performed by untrained witch doctors—that is, ritual practitioners mixing unhygienic concoctions for use on poorly educated, impoverished people who have no other options. In spite of such images, however, traditional medicine has been on the upswing in recent years. Many studies have shown that traditional medicines do exist in a wide variety of cultures, including one study that concluded that 38 percent of Americans were using some sort of complementary or alternative medicine in 2007 (Barnes et al. 2008). A similar study conducted in urban Nigeria found that herbal medicines are used by 66.8 percent of the population (Oreagba et al. 2011).

Togo is one of the least economically developed countries in West Africa and one in which herbal medicine use is widespread. Thus, its national health care system should have much to gain by incorporating village medicines into its practice. Nevertheless, as of today, public biomedical hospitals typically do not recognize village medicines as a complementary form of healing; doctors are often irked when they see patients who have put off biomedical care while trying a home-brewed remedy. Nothing is taught about the herbal system of healing in Togolese medical school, and many doctors graduate with knowledge only of the side effects that can follow from the use of non-pharmaceuticals. While it is known that traditional medicines have a high prevalence in rural areas where biomedical care is often more difficult to access, little is known about its prevalence and use in Togolese urban centers.

Methodology

My research sought to ask what role local medicines play in an urban center where both biomedical and traditional options are available. When do people use them and for what illnesses? How long do people typically delay biomedical care and why? At the start of my research, I had to specify the type of traditional medicine I would survey. Would it include the omnipotent powders in bottles made from dried leaves and bark? Would it include the surprising number of Chinese medicines sold in stores scattered around the city? Would it also include those plants sold in stores that were advertised as coming from Europe? Would it include the medicines of *guérisseurs* (healers) and ritual specialists? Given the limited time frame of my research, I decided to define traditional medicine as plant-based healing that had origins in local culture. This definition was consistent with previous research (Oreagba et al. 2011) and allowed me to focus primarily on the plants and their derivatives sold in markets and throughout the streets of the city (although other forms of traditional medicine were ubiquitous and unavoidable).

To sample a cross section of the city, I conducted interviews with fifty people, randomly selected, in three geographically and culturally distinct neighborhoods,[1] as well as with fifty patients, again randomly selected, in the hospital where I served as an intern. I also conducted interviews with a wide range of professionals involved in health care, including an official with the Department of Health, doctors at private and public clinics, pharmacists, a diviner, medical students, and women selling traditional medicines in the market. While the interviews conducted randomly throughout the city were used to collect prevalence statistics, the health-focused interviews were used to gain general knowledge about the types of traditional medicines being used and the interactions between the biomedical and traditional systems. The majority of the interviews were conducted as guided conversations, in which I started the interview by posing a few questions and then followed the thread of the conversation.

One of the most valuable lessons I learned while conducting this research came in an interview on July 4, about two weeks before the end of my stay, with a renowned tele-diviner. As we were sitting on his porch, munching homemade *frites* (potato fries) and discussing his clients, he casually mentioned calls he got from the Bè hospital's birthing unit. Even though all forms of traditional medicine are banned on hospital property, the nurses and midwives would call him during difficult births and ask him to perform a short ritual for the suffering mother from his office about thirty minutes outside the city. This was the same birthing unit in which I had spent my first week of research shadowing, where all of the nurses and midwives I spoke with vehemently insisted that inside the hospital they relied only on "hospital" medicine. Of course, I should not have expected that after a week these nurses were going to tell a foreigner that they were breaking hospital policy. Still, the jolt I received from this insight made me realize I needed to be careful about drawing conclusions from a single set of conversations or observations. Several days later, I ran into a woman secretly selling her traditional *pomades* (lotions)—said to cure everything from dry skin to breast cancer—to patients in the hospital's waiting room. I suspected that these two incidents represented only a small portion of the traditional medicine that was actually being transacted within the hospital, transactions about which I was entirely unaware at the time.

Initial Research Findings

One cool, rainy afternoon as I was randomly selecting interview subjects with my translator, Georges, we stumbled upon a woman sitting next to what looked very much like a Gatorade cooler. Georges suggested the vendor might be a good interview subject as he nonchalantly bought a cup of her murky-looking liquid. I peered suspiciously into the mug he was handed and saw what appeared to be warmed water, mixed with a little mud. As all eyes honed in on me, searching for a reaction, I was offered a taste (with Georges assuring me that it would not be offensive if I did not swallow). Every instinct (and global health class) told me to say no, but at the same time that cup of goodness-knows-what was my project for the summer, and what better way was there to conduct research than through firsthand experience—what the anthropologists call "participant observation"? I took a sip and instantly, due to its intense bitterness, spat it back out.

What is traditional medicine? Loquaciously defined in Togolese law, it is "the assembly of all knowledge, techniques of preparation and utilization of substances, measures and practices of use, explainable or not by the modern state of science, which are based on the collective Togolese sociocultural and religious foundations, drawing on lived experiences and observations passed from generation to generation and which serve to diagnose, prevent or eliminate an imbalance of physical, mental, social or spiritual well-being."[2] This description encompasses all types of healers: herbalists, psychotherapists, ritualists, phlebotomists, midwives, and more. Many of the people I interviewed considered this holistic healing approach, discussed later, a very attractive quality.

Overall, everyone with whom I spoke in Lomé had used herbal medicine at some point in his or her life, a phenomenon never previously noted in an urban area. While only 77 percent (N = 100) had used an herbal treatment within the previous six months, virtually everyone had exposure to plant-based remedies growing up as a child—including those who had spent their entire lives in the city. Common reasons cited for less frequent use of childhood treatments included a dislike of the taste, fear of the side effects, lack of recent illness to treat, and the presence of a physician in the family who cared for family members at his or her biomedical practice.

There were three groups of illnesses for which the subjects I interviewed would cite greater use of traditional medicines. One was *palu* (short for *paludisme*, French for malaria). Palu seemed to be a type of cover category that encompassed not just malaria but almost any type of illness for which the symptoms included a headache and fever. Another comprised everyday maladies such as stomachaches, fatigue, menstruation, and hangovers for which a visit to the doctor was not deemed necessary. Similar to Americans who will pop an Advil or take extra vitamin C, Togolese will self-treat with medicinal tea, often made from tree leaves growing in their inner courtyards. One interviewee speculated that due to the starch-heavy diet of the Togolese, every household has a traditional cure for hemorrhoids growing on hand. The final class of illnesses comprised those that people believed biomedicine could not cure—"African" illnesses such as yellow fever and anemia, as well as those more difficult to treat illnesses such as infertility,

4.1 A list of illnesses treated set outside a shop selling traditional medicine in Lomé.

epilepsy, and HIV/AIDS. In these instances, many people insisted, traditional medicines were the only route to take, because hospital-prescribed remedies had failed them.

The most common method for taking traditional medicines was as a tisane, an herbal tea, measured in a small cup three times a day (always "after the sun comes up and before the sun goes down"). While it was fairly common to see the leaves and bark for these tisanes sold in the markets, it was just as common to see the pre-brewed mixtures sold on the streets. The giant orange coolers, such as the one I mentioned earlier, always seemed to pop up early in the morning for breakfast, or late in the afternoon just as everyone was leaving work. These "pre-brews" were especially popular among the motorcycle taxi drivers, who claimed they were perfect for relieving the muscle soreness and fatigue brought on by driving the bumpy, unpaved roads. Others I interviewed also demonstrated their use of vapors, suppositories, and body washes, each method specific to a certain illness, with its own type of dosage.

Only 51 percent (N = 61) of the interview participants with children professed to current usage of herbal medicine with their children, reflecting a difference in medical choice between oneself and one's children. Many claimed this was due to the fact that children disliked the bitter taste (I can empathize!) and because they did not understand how to properly adjust the dosage. While shadowing in the hospital, I also observed much more caution taken with children, as hospital appointments were made for "maladies" such as that of a healthy baby losing weight the first two days after it was born—a common phenomenon. My host mother also asked me whether she should take her young daughter to the pediatrician after observing a small bump on her head. Using the small amount of medical knowledge I had, I reassured her it was just like the twenty-five mosquito bites I had on my legs and her daughter would probably be fine. Overall, these interviews appeared to suggest that the hospital was the more trusted health resource when children fell ill (assuming people had the money to afford hospital care).

Decision Making

Why are people in a modern city using traditional medicines when they have access to both traditional and biomedical healing systems? Many factors are involved.

First, there was the issue of money. Many of those I interviewed were wary of the monetary consequences of a hospital visit. For instance, here is a typical hospital visit for a man who suspects he has malaria. The patient arrives at the hospital as early as 7 AM, often by motorcycle with a family member or friend, to pay the consultation fee of 1,000 CFA francs and ensure that he will get his name recorded so he can see the doctor before lunchtime.[3] By 9 AM, the patient will be called in to have his vitals checked: his temperature taken with a thermometer he provides (available for purchase at the hospital pharmacy) and his blood pressure measured with a stethoscope and cuff. Then he will go back to the waiting room for another half-hour or so before being called to see a doctor—or, in some cases, a physician's assistant or nurse—who will require a 50 CFA franc fee for the glove used for the physical examination. If the patient is developing a severe case of malaria (or another serious illness), he is immediately asked to pre-pay a 5,000 CFA franc ($10) five-day bed fee. Finally, if meds are prescribed and in stock, he (or family members) will have to consider whether they can afford them. Some pharmacists I interviewed said it was not uncommon to have people come in asking for prescription medicines without a prescription—that they could afford the medicine or the consultation for the prescription, but not both. Considering that the patient and his accompanying family members or friends were not working for the day (or more) spent in the hospital—thus losing income—it is easy to understand how such costs exceed the means of many urban dwellers. And for many I interviewed, it was considered taboo to set money aside for emergency illness, as that might invite illness to strike the family. The alternative, herbal medicines, seemed awfully appealing in contrast to this: the women selling herbs would provide a quick consultation for free if the patient needed it, and the plants would cost 50–500 CFA francs, depending on the season. And no extra time off was taken from work, as the plants needed could be found without any wait at the local market.

Second was the issue of habit and tradition. While many of those interviewed stated that they used traditional medicines because they were short on money, many said they would still use traditional medicine if they had unlimited monetary resources. Why? Not only because it was what they knew and understood but also because the medicine is effective. Thirty-four out of the first thirty-five people interviewed said their parents had given them herbal medicine when they were children, and the primary source of knowledge of plant species and dosages was from parents. Rarely did an interview subject say his mother explained what she was doing when he got sick; rather, most of the knowledge gained was through observation. If there was uncertainty about what herb to take when an illness arose, it was common to ask a neighbor, an older relative within the homestead, or the women selling the plants for advice. In this way, the city itself became a general fund of knowledge, via word of mouth, to which everybody had access if he or she inquired. Often, the type of plant taken also had an aesthetic connection to the illness—red bark or leaves were used to treat maladies of the blood (such as anemia); yellow bark was used for palu or fever (which can produce jaundice). This aesthetic connection was comforting for many, as it made more cultural sense than taking an indistinguishable white pill that appeared to cure everything. Many traditional plants were also integrated into local cuisine: "anti-biotique," a leafy sauce on the menu in most fufu (food) bars, was known to be effective against stomachache and parasites.[4] Above all, we must assume that these rural medicines are efficacious. Why otherwise would they have lasted for hundreds of years and be so widely consumed today?

The third issue was the ease with which traditional plants can be accessed. Throughout interviews, subjects often would go to nearby trees and pick off the leaves, all the while explaining the unique (and often numerous) medicinal properties each plant held. Many families also had stores of medicinal plants in their homestead, brought back from the rural villages where they had visited family or friends. If the plants needed could not be found within the homestead proper, it was easy to go out in the morning and find women walking through the streets with large baskets of assorted leaves, roots, and bark on top of their heads. Finally, if the patient still could not find what he or she needed, all of the local markets had several options. In the Grand Marché, Lomé's largest market, many stands had more than a hundred different specimens, each with unique curative properties. One of the vendors in the marketplace informed me that the majority of her customers treated their visits like a hospital consultation or a visit to a pharmacy: they would tell her their symptoms, and she would tell them what to buy. She would also take orders ahead of time and prepare bundles of herbs for specific illnesses, as well as bundles for the sellers of the tisanes on the side of the road. The knowledge base required for this work is mind-boggling; the woman interviewed had been selling

4.2 One of many medicine stands in Lomé's Grand Marché.

plants from 6 AM to 6 PM six days a week for more than forty-five years. She was currently apprenticing one of her daughters into the business—its own type of medical education.

Finally, part of the reason for the staying power of traditional medicines in the city has to do with the holistic nature of the system in which they are embedded. While many plants were prescribed to treat bodily symptoms, they did wonders for the mind, as well. For many, it was comforting to know these plants had been around for ages and were the same medicines their forebears had used. In contrast to white powders made up of foreign chemicals, prescribed natural products, such as leaves and bark, seemed more reassuring and more efficacious. One interview subject professed that he found traditional tisanes to be especially satisfying because they would induce urination, which, he felt, indicated a cleansing of the body from the illness and harmful chemicals from medicines. Many also believed biomedical treatments could not cure certain supernatural afflictions—epilepsy and psychosis in particular. I witnessed firsthand a young baby seizing in the pediatric ward of the hospital, and although the doctor on call instantly prescribed diazepam, the hospital pharmacy was all out. This unavailability of medicines in combination with a local belief in spirits made traditional healers a more trusted source for immediate treatment. Moreover, while Western doctors are not able to give a definitive diagnosis for psychosis, as there is often no underlying physical condition, diviners or "charlatans" are sometimes able to get to the root of the mental suffering, providing the cure the afflicted seek. In Western society, this role is largely left to psychologists.

While taking all of these advantages of traditional medicine into account, the decision-making process for those who fell ill still was not always simple. While traditional medicines have many advantages, they are not always the first choice for care. Some interviewees were concerned that traditional healers did not differentiate between the dosages given to different patients (of different size or age) and worried about the side effects of overdose—mentioning hepatitis and pancreatitis as possible side effects. The Togolese government has also recently placed a ban on the advertisement of traditional medical practices, hoping to discourage not so much the use of traditional medicines as the market in false practitioners, or "charlatans." As a result, there is more secrecy and less free conversation about herbal medicine today.

The most common health-care path I observed was one that used both traditional and biomedical methods, but at separate times. When someone fell ill—whether it was from fatigue, headache, or fever—she would typically start with some sort of herbal medicine. If she was still ill after taking this treatment (over the course of two days to a week), she would go to the public hospital for a diagnosis or prescription. Filling prescriptions would be the next step if she could afford it on top of the hospital fees. However, the diagnosis often would be taken straight back to a healer to ask for a more informed traditional cure. Using both systems of treatment simultaneously was usually avoided, as people wanted to see whether one would work before trying the other.

Future Directions

What will be the future of traditional medicines in Lomé? When asked whether traditional medicines will become less prevalent in the future, twenty-seven interviewees said no, while thirty-six said yes (ten said it depended on the future actions of the government). Those who said herbal medicines would remain as prevalent as they currently are often cited the economic status of the country and the habitual nature behind the usage of many traditional plants. Also, many responded that if the cures work against everyday palu, why should they be eliminated?

Those who predicted a decrease in the use of traditional medicines had a much broader range of concerns, often relating to how the younger generation is today being socialized. First, they claimed, was the fact that knowledge is no longer conveyed between parents and children, as it was before. As an example, I was surprised when young adults were able to tell me that one should take traditional medicine before the sun went down, but they were not sure why.[5] Others expressed concern about the ban on advertising, saying that televisions, radios, and newspapers now played an integral part in the decisions of young people; if the youth were exposed only to advertisements for biomedical treatments, they would be more likely to choose biomedical treatments. Traditional medicines were also not covered in the University of Lomé medical school curriculum, and three individuals I interviewed cited discontinued use after their (biomedically) educated children advised them against it. Finally, there was the black market in pharmaceuticals—of packaged medicines found on practically every street corner in the city. They consisted of expired products from Europe and the United States and unregulated medicines made in factories in Nigeria and India. Despite their potential negative consequences, these medicines were cheap compared with those sold by the pharmacies, and many people found them useful for easing pain and were taking them instead of traditional plants. This raises the question of whether black market pharmaceuticals will replace traditional medicines for a certain demographic of young users.

Overall, this information highlights the malleable future of traditional medicines and the constantly evolving mind-set surrounding them.

Remaining Questions

While this study has underscored the prevalence of traditional medicines in a modern West African city, many of those interviewed expressed concerns about the ways in which traditional and biomedical health care should interact going forward. When should an individual use which one? Is it safe to use both forms of medicine at the same time? Should the individual just stick with what he or she knows will work? These types of questions suggest three areas of future research: how collaboration between the old and new health-care systems could occur; what the efficacy and toxicity of the most prevalent traditional treatments are relative to their biomedical counterparts; and, finally, how the public could be better educated about their options. Research on all three of these fronts would be beneficial for the nation, enabling choices to be made about the optimization of the two systems in play.

Research on how the professionals of the two systems could collaborate in future endeavors, rather than existing in neighborly exclusivity, would ameliorate health care overall within the city. Both biomedical and traditional healers need to be able to admit there are certain illnesses they do not have the ability to cure, especially in a low-income setting, and they should be able to provide referrals to one another. While at present it is common for patients to choose to go back and forth between the two systems, one does not often hear biomedical doctors in public clinics supporting patients' decisions to see traditional healers. Collaboration would thus involve working with government officials, biomedical health-care providers, and bodies of traditional healers to create a system in which partnership would be safe and efficient, always putting the needs of the patient first. One traditional healer I interviewed shared her experience working in Gabon: once a month, government officials would allow certified traditional healers to go into the hospitals and see the patients who were not responding to biomedical treatment. While they were not paid much (3,000 CFA francs, or $6, for the day), the government would also sponsor a dinner for all of the healers. She cited this system as being advantageous for all involved—after all, why should the hospital not give the patients every opportunity for a cure? Similar options for collaboration in Lomé might be worth exploring.

The second research question examines which traditional treatments are effective and safe, especially if they are being taken at the same time as biomedical pharmaceuticals. Such research could provide a scientific basis so that biomedical doctors feel more confident referring care to traditional healers. While some worry about the toxicity of traditional plants, especially when dosages are not monitored—although research needs to be done to know more—others complain about delays that occur in seeking biomedical care while trying herbal medicines that may not work on a given disease. Many also said that traditional remedies can cause complications (especially to kidney and liver) if they are not taken properly. While little scientific research has been carried out on these medicines, this may be starting to change. Two local research centers have started their own investigations of certain compounds, including CERFOPLAM (the Center of Research and Training on Curative Plants) at the University of Lomé and the Centre Omnitherapeutique Africain, located outside the city. The research these centers are conducting is important for building the confidence of the public and creating a traditional system that makes the most of modern resources, allowing patients to be well informed about the risks and benefits.

Finally, all of this information needs to be better communicated to physicians, healers, and, especially, the public. At the moment, the government of Togo has only one member of the Ministry of Health responsible for overseeing the practice of traditional medicine throughout the country. If he does not even have enough funding to print copies of the law regarding the practice of traditional medicine, how is he supposed to be responsible for creating public awareness about educated medical decision making? Some patients also do not understand how taking both types of medicine at the same time could have negative consequences. I heard about more than one patient taking tisanes at the same time they were taking medicine provided by the hospital so that, they claimed, they would flush out any "bad" chemicals through frequent urination. Obviously, this could also mean flushing out the hospital medications before they could have any effect on the illness. Others do not understand the dosages of traditional medicines they are supposed to give to children and spend money on hospital visits instead of using the herbal remedies that they know to work on themselves. Public hospitals, with government and administrative approval and financial support, could start education campaigns that address not only the risks but also the benefits of traditional herbal remedies and how they can be used safely and effectively to complement biomedical care.

Conclusion

The use of traditional medicine remains remarkably prevalent throughout the urban metropolis of Lomé. In interviews with more than one hundred residents throughout the city, including physicians, patients, and lawmakers, I discovered that virtually everybody I spoke with had used plant-based remedies at some point in his or her life. Furthermore, more than three-quarters of those I interviewed had used an herbal treatment in the preceding six months. While certain classes of illnesses—including everyday aches, pains, and fever, as well as difficult-to-treat maladies such as HIV/AIDS and infertility—were more prone to inspire herbal medicine use than others, choosing between traditional and biomedical healing systems was not always a straightforward decision. Often, people reported that they not only thought about their available financial resources but also considered family traditions and the ease of access to and holistic nature of the chosen treatment. Those interviewed remained divided when predicting how the prevalence of traditional medicine may change going forward, highlighting the unpredictability of herbal medicine's future in this setting. I believe that much work remains to be done in Lomé so that these two forms of medicine—biomedical and traditional—can safely coexist.

Notes

1. The neighborhoods included Bè, Adewi, and Kodjoviakope.
2. Togolese Law no. 2001–017, Relative to the Practice of Traditional Medicine in Togo, 2001, art. 17.
3. At the time of my visit, the conversion rate was approximately 500 CFA francs to $1. That amount will buy three kilograms of rice or feed someone for several days (Taondyande et al. 2011). A common salary, for those lucky enough to work for wages, is $50 (25,000 CFA francs) a month: "Salaires minimums au Togo à partir du 01–01–2012," Votresalarie.org, Togo, WageIndicator Network, March 3, 2014, http://www.votresalaire.org/togo/home/salaire/salaire-minimum-tarifs. However, many individuals, including street vendors, earn much less. For comparison, a consultation at a private clinic cost about 7,500 CFA francs, and a consultation at a home clinic cost about 500 CFA francs.
4. Despite the addition of the same leaves used in many traditional tisanes for stomachaches—afiti for digestion, agnoto for cramps—interview subjects were surprised when I inquired about the sauces, because they did not consider them medicine, even though they called one of their favorite sauces "anti-biotique." It seemed that some were more willing to consume the leaves in sauces than to take them in other, more medically oriented concoctions.
5. I found out from an older man, however, that after sundown certain flowers "go to sleep" and become less effective medications.

References

Barnes, Patricia M., Barbara Bloom, and Richard L. Nahin. 2008. *Complementary and Alternative Medicine Use among Adults and Children: 2007.* U.S. National Health Statistics Reports no. 12. Hyattsville, MD: National Center for Health Statistics.

Oreagba, Ibrahim, Kazeem Adeola Oshikoya, and Mercy Amachree. 2011. "Herbal Medicine Use among Urban Residents in Lagos, Nigeria." *BMC Complementary and Alternative Medicine* 11: 117.

Taondyande, Maurice, Momar Sylla, and Songré Oumarou. 2011. "Dynamique de la consommation alimentaire et la hausse des prix dans la sous-région Ouest-Africaine: Togo." http://fsg.afre.msu.edu/srai/Togo_Raport_Consom_final.pdf.

Vickers, Andrew, Catherine Zollman, and Roberta Lee. 2001. "Herbal Medicine." *Western Journal of Medicine* 175, no. 2: 125–28.

World Health Organization. 2013. *WHO Traditional Medicine Strategy, 2014–2023.* Geneva: World Health Organization.

5. Village Health Insurance
Cheyenne Allenby

"Without this system, I would not have been able to bring my family to the clinic and buy medicine" was a sentence repeated again and again in interviews about the viability of a community health insurance system created by Duke students in 2008 in the village of Kuwdé. Under the plan, families pay a small sum (1,800 CFA francs, or about $3.60) to enter the program and receive free consultations and subsidized medicine. The scheme's success was evident in the records of the health clinic for which the system was created, showing increased visits and large savings for enrolled members. Most significant, the program was completely self-sustaining. My research sought to carry out a comprehensive overview of this insurance system's successes and failures and to assess whether the model developed in Kuwdé is one that might travel to other villages in Togo and beyond. I found that despite initial success, positive feedback, and sustainability, many families in the community were not enrolling in the program, and some families had left it altogether. In what follows, I explore some of the reasons for this surprising turn of events, as well as the pros and cons of the health insurance scheme.

Background

Only 25 percent of Togo's population has access to biomedical health services. One of the major reasons for such unequal access is people's inability to afford the cost of medicine (Sala-Diakanda et al. 2006). For rural villages in the central region of Togo, earnings are less than $1 a day; only 30 percent of people have access to potable water; only 20 percent have access to health care; and infant mortality is 141 per 1,000 births. In addition, the malaria morbidity rate among children younger than five is 66 percent (Sala-Diakanda et al. 2006). In Togo as a whole, there is but one medical doctor for every 11,171 inhabitants and one community health leader for every 10,000 inhabitants.

The availability of health care has been greatly affected by political "decentralization." Administrative decentralization in Togo began in the mid-1990s and was seen as an accompaniment to neoliberal policies of privatization, marketization, and democratic governance (Bonnal n.d.). Through decentralization, decision making and the implementation of development initiatives were to be shared with villages and localities, and centralized state services (and some monies) were to be redistributed. However, Togo's limited resources have meant that decentralization is more often a burden on the local than a help. Few state monies flow through the health system and development sector these days, and clinics, communities, and regions are left to fend for themselves. As a result, the government no longer subsidizes the health services and medicine it previously did, and health care has been compromised for many individuals, such as those in Kuwdé.

In Kara, the region in which Kuwdé is located, the child mortality rate is 144 per 1,000 (Ministry of Health 2001). This is worse than the average for Togo because it is the poorest region, has lower effective health service coverage, is in mountainous terrain with an inadequate road system, and has poor water and sanitation. Kara benefits the least from bilateral and multilateral assistance to the health sector. The leading causes of mortality for children younger than five are malaria, diarrhea, measles, malnutrition, and respiratory disease. Approximately 73 percent of children younger than sixteen months in Togo are anemic. The most pressing issues include vitamin A deficiency, protein energy malnutrition, and anemia. Drug availability is a top priority for health care providers.

The health-care system in Togo operates on three levels—community, district, and regional—and Kuwdé's Case de Santé (Health Hut) is the lowest level, running on a shoestring budget (raised by charging extra money for medicine) and staffed by health workers trained through short (two-week) internships. Still, the workers are dedicated and over time acquire hands-on skill in treating sickness. In neighboring Farendé, the district administrative center, a second-level clinic, the Centre Médico-Sociale (CMS), somewhere between a big clinic and a small hospital, serves a large multi-village population. It is staffed by twelve salaried workers, paid in part by the state and in part by a Swiss nongovernmental organization (NGO) and overseen by a young, energetic "medical assistant." At the highest level are regional hospitals, supported by the state and serving large populations.

Kuwdé's Case de Santé was founded in 1998 and is currently run by two medical assistants, Basil and Odile. Both are in charge of consultations, births, prenatal consultations, and the distribution of medicine. When necessary—when they are unable to treat a case—they will refer it to the neighboring health center in Farendé. The clinic provides care to anyone in the village, as well as to those from neighboring villages who seek care, and in so doing alleviates the burden on the larger health clinic in Farendé. In addition to births, the most frequent maladies the clinic treats are malaria, anemia, and dysentery. The clinic provides medicine such as amoxicillin,

5.1 The Case de Santé, renovated in 2011 with support from the Noar Foundation, an American NGO.

ibuprofen, antimalarials, quinine, and Bactrim, which it purchases from a religious NGO or from pharmacies. The insurance program was founded in 2008, and in 2012 it had eighteen member families with an average of eight family members each.

Methodology

Over the course of two months in the summer of 2012, I conducted research for this study. I used semi-structured interviews combined with informal conversations and observations. I spent mornings at the Case de Santé in Kuwdé in conversation with the two health workers and reviewing data in their consultation logs. I observed consultations and medicine distribution and sometimes traveled with the health workers to the homesteads of families and healers.

Interviews and Observations at the Clinic

I interviewed the two medical workers at the Case de Santé and asked them to describe common procedures in assessing and treating patients. I also asked about the training they receive and their relation to other clinics in nearby villages. I posed additional questions about disease, prescribed medication, and record keeping to fully understand how the clinic functioned and treated certain sicknesses or referred them to the larger clinic in Farendé. The goal of these interviews was to find out more about the general practice of health care in the area, with the aim of assessing the health insurance scheme that Duke students had created. I also witnessed routine consultations.

Health Insurance Data

A lot of my time was spent with the health assistants going over the data of consultations for the insured, such as total number of consultations in the course of the year and the amount of money spent following these consultations. In addition, I collected data on the number of prescriptions filled for those who were insured, medications purchased, and which village families were coming for care. Most important, I compared the data for families enrolled in the system with those not enrolled.

5.2 Basile and Odile helping me with the figures.

Interviews at Homesteads

Interviews were conducted with the aid of the health assistants at the homesteads of families enrolled in the system, those not enrolled in the system, and those who had joined but had subsequently dropped out. Questions were posed about general understanding of the health-care system, usage of traditional medicine, thoughts about the insurance program, and understanding of community-based health care and preventative health. In addition, I asked what improvements they wanted to see in the clinic and in the insurance program to assess what would encourage families to either enroll in the program or maintain enrollment status.

Informal Conversations

Less formal conversations with villagers were held during non-work hours, at community gatherings, and in the homestead where I lived and ate meals. People were extremely forthcoming in sharing their thoughts about sickness and health, local medicine, and the relationship between the state and health care. I found these conversations useful in thinking through issues surrounding the insurance program.

Initial Findings

Consultations and Purchases of Medicine Have Increased

During the first year that the clinic was founded (1998), it had 120 consultations. When I arrived at the clinic at the end of May in 2012, it had already conducted 370 consultations—in less than half a year. In addition, the purchasing of medicine has increased by more than 100,000 CFA francs ($200) since 2005, a not insignificant amount for villagers living on $1 a week. While this increase is correlated with the increase in the number of consultations at the clinic, the cause of the consultation increase is unclear and likely due to multiple factors, including increased health awareness (clinic workers today engage in publicity campaigns, going from homestead to homestead several times a year), the fact that the insurance scheme has been around for several years, and recent improvements to the clinic made by a Duke student's father (adding solar-powered electricity, hot water, latrines, and showers).

The Current Insurance Scheme Is Sustainable

As mentioned above, families can enroll in the insurance plan for 1,800 CFA francs ($3.60) per year, in return for which the consultation fee is waived and medicine can be purchased at one-quarter the retail price. On average, an insured family visited 5.5 times a year and spent 240 CFA francs each visit on medicine at the subsidized rate.

Although I was unable to measure quantifiable improvements to health in the community resulting from families' participation in the insurance scheme, interviews revealed that families were highly appreciative and felt that its presence had benefited not only their families, even saving lives, but also the larger community.

Should the program continue as it has in the past, with families purchasing on average the same amount of medicine, it should be sustainable. That is, the plan is currently bringing in more money each year through enrollment fees than it is losing in making up for lost revenues from the discounted medicine. (The clinic doubles the purchase price of medicines when selling to those not in the insurance system while halving the purchase price for those who are insured.) Still, it is hard to say whether the system will continue to net a profit each year. This will depend on family need and on how much medicine insured people buy. An additional limitation to sustainability could be that the program does not cap the number of family members figured by homestead, which often includes extended family members. Currently, the program is rolling over profits into the next year.

Benefits of Health Care

I found that despite the robust nature of Kuwdé's "traditional" medical system (see Middleton and Rotolo, this volume), people were also readily accessing health care from the local clinic and understood the importance of the insurance system. Many families I interviewed expressed gratitude for the opportunity to join the system because it provided health care they had not previously been able to afford. For example, one of the large families I interviewed who had used the clinic more than any other enrolled family acknowledged that the insurance program enabled them to send their children to the clinic right away and purchase medicine. This allowed for a quicker recovery and for the children to continue to go to school and work in the fields. Because of the insurance program, this family was able to receive 20,000 CFA francs ($40) in consultations and medicine for approximately 5,000 CFA francs ($10) after paying the insurance fee—for a savings of 15,000 CFA francs ($30).

This father of five said it was his children who used the clinic the most (while he often sought help from a traditional healer for his ailments, including anemia). Another father insisted that despite using traditional medicine for pain and spiritual ailments, his family readily attended the clinic, thanks to the benefits provided by the insurance system. A third family explained they were able to buy more prescribed medicine because of the prices under the insurance system and otherwise would not have gone to the Case de Santé at all.

Relationship to Neighboring Villages

The Kuwdé Case de Santé receives patients from the surrounding area, including Boa, Katchalikaté, and Farendé-haut. Although this was not recorded in the ledger, interviews revealed that patients from Tchikawa were coming to the Case de Santé, as well, despite the presence of a similar clinic in their community. The largest number of patients come from Boa, the large three-quartier village that surrounds the Case de Santé, and from the quartier of Kuwdé, which borders the clinic. Many of the patients, including pregnant women, had traveled considerable distances, indexing the quality of care offered at the clinic.

Importantly, the Case de Santé alleviates the burden of cases at the CMS in Farendé. François, the medical assistant at the Farendé CMS, described the Case de Santé as the first step in seeking care and a filter for sick people who otherwise would have to travel to Farendé to be treated. The Case de Santé can refer people it cannot treat to the clinic in Farendé but otherwise helps in alleviating the burden of anemia, dysentery, pain, and malaria cases on the clinic in Farendé.

Discussion

Through interviews and observations at the clinic, I found that community sentiments reflected the success apparent in the data. Interviewees spoke positively about the clinic's coexistence with traditional medicine, about the benefits of clinic health care for their children, and about saving money through the insurance scheme. Individuals in the community, as well as the two health assistants, were eager to highlight improvements that could be made and possible reasons that more families are not enrolled in the system.

The Insurance Scheme Can Coexist with Traditional Medicine

Many of the families interviewed use both the clinic and the local medical system. The clinic was primarily used to treat diseases such as dysentery and malaria, with interviewees saying that they found the clinic's medicine especially effective for these two maladies. I also found that when people suffered pain from working in the fields (aches, soreness) or exhaustion from the sun, many preferred the clinic. One interviewee described going to traditional healers for "spiritual" ailments that were "thrown" at him by other people and thus had to be treated by a diviner (who can determine mystical causation), while he and family members readily attended the clinic for other sicknesses. People also came to the clinic after traditional medicines did not relieve their symptoms. No interviewee expressed skepticism about the insurance program (with its biomedicine) existing alongside local healers, but some felt that healers overreached by claiming to be able to cure everything (but not in fact being able to do so), and medical assistants were concerned about healers' knowledge about dosage (how much to prescribe or how to modulate dosage according to the age and size of the patient). Overall, the interviewees did not hesitate to discuss the compatibility between traditional medicine and clinic medicine and did not express any concern about how they or others in the community felt about going to both the clinic and local healers.

The Insurance Scheme and Children

Many heads of families said that the insurance plan provided care for their children that they otherwise would not have been able to afford. One family head said that a big advantage to being insured was that he could send his children to the clinic as soon as they got sick, rather than waiting to see whether their malady got better on its own before deciding to spend his money on treatment. Of course, when children are treated quickly, sickness will not spread from child to child. The clinic's books reveal that children make up a big percentage of total consultations, which fits with what I saw when I was at the clinic: dozens of children coming for treatment.

Families Save Money

All families enrolled in the insurance plan said they saved money. Had they not been enrolled, the cost of consultations and the extra money paid for medicines would have exceeded the price of the insurance buy-in. Another saving is that insured families can go to the clinic immediately, thus nipping a disease in the bud and avoiding having to make more visits and buy more medicine in the long term. (As mentioned above, families not in the system often waited longer to treat their children—to see whether they would be cured naturally or through the use of traditional medicines—to save money.) I found that bigger families saved the most money, and interviews with those families revealed that they were aware of this benefit.

Why Not More Families?

The largest puzzle in all of this is that more families are not enrolled. Why, if there are clear health and financial benefits to all who are enrolled—as attested to by interviews with those in the system—are only eighteen out of three hundred families enrolled in the insurance plan? A range of reasons appear to account for this situation.

First, this is a desperately poor area, with people juggling their limited means throughout the year. In addition to having to feed and clothe large families (the common family size is eight to ten people), they have to pay school fees for their children, buy beer for workgroups, and finance funeral and initiation ceremonies, among other expenditures. While health is at the top of the list, it may at times take a back seat to other demands, if only because the money is already gone when someone gets sick. Or a head of family may choose to go to a traditional healer instead of going to the clinic to access cheaper medicine and avoid having to pay for treatment ahead of time (with healers, payment occurs in the form of beer or a chicken *after* health is regained). The clinic is also associated with high and sometimes superfluous expenditure: medicine is often prescribed in bundles, which can inflate the amount a treatment should cost. For example, paracetamol may be prescribed in addition to an antibiotic to help with pain, while the antibiotic is what is really necessary. Finally, the clinic is equipped to handle less complex diagnoses such as malaria, anemia, and pain. When more complex medical issues are in play, people have to go to the CMS in Farendé or the hospital in Paguda and may wish to save their money for such occasions.

Second, when the program was first implemented, insurance payments were due at the end of August, because that is when the Duke students who designed the system were in Kuwdé (and they wanted to see it up and running before their departure). As we later found out, however, that start date coincides with the beginning of classes, and parents were hard-pressed to pay school fees and insurance at the same time. Therefore, we decided to switch the insurance start time to January 1, after the November harvest when families have more cash in hand. (Today, the start date is more flexible, with families joining whenever they want during the year.)

Finally, the idea of insurance is not familiar to farmers in this area. The idea of spending money now for gains in the future is not an easy one to grasp. Nor is the idea of improving the health of the village—paying into a common fund—a familiar concept for people in this area. Moreover, one man stated that he worried that paying now for a future sickness might in and of itself make him sick. Another asked whether he could get his money back if he paid into the insurance scheme but never got sick during the year. We in the United States are so used to the idea of insurance that we take it for granted. But the Togolese still find the concept strange.

For all of these reasons, rather than because of distrust or hostility, the insurance system has not yet fully caught on.

Improvements

Aware of the system's shortcomings, and aiming to get more families to join, we proposed some changes to the insurance program.

In addition to changing the start date (first from September 1 to January 1, then to any time throughout the year), to allow insured families to pay premiums when they are more likely to have cash in hand, we instituted a small rebate (300 CFA francs) for those who did not fall sick (and never went to the clinic) during the year. The rebate was a response to complaints from people who failed to understand the benefits of joining a future-based insurance plan, under which you may or may not get sick but have to pay into the plan nevertheless.

We also suggested improvements to the accounting system so that the benefits (and deficits) of the insurance scheme can be better tracked. As of summer 2012, insurance figures for all families enrolled in the system were kept in a notebook separate from the general ledger. The larger ledger records all consultations, and a separate notebook records pharmaceutical expenditures (including expenses and gains for each month). Duke students made suggestions to improve the efficiency of recordkeeping to also make reviewing the data easier in future years. Accurate bookkeeping should enable medical assistants to assess the program's well-being and give them access to information they can use to persuade families to join the program.[1] It will also enable them easily to show members how much they have saved by being in the system.

Finally, we suggested that the two Case de Santé health workers engage in more outreach so that families are better informed about the benefits of the insurance scheme. Every year, Duke students and the two health workers have convened a meeting of the whole community to discuss and advertise the insurance plan. But it is probably a mistake to assume that a general meeting like this is all that is needed (and people will come running). In fact, individual families may need more information than is disseminated in a group context, and house visits may be more appropriate ways to convey that information. Local families may also appreciate a more personalized approach.

Two years after I left, a Duke student came up with an even better idea: going door to door to show each insured family how much it had saved that year in paying for medicine. Having these figures concretely in mind—the student gave the families a sheet of paper with figures—seemed to make a difference for people who are not in the habit of running year-end figures of expenditures. The student also ran the numbers for those who had gone to the clinic but were uninsured to show them how much they would have saved if they had been insured. Within two months, thirty new families had signed up (out of a total of three hundred), tripling the number of insured families almost overnight. While this increase was largely thanks to the student's clever idea to make savings more visible and known to patients, it was likely also due to the fact that a small medical team, with a visiting student, showed up at the homestead to try to persuade families to join. This personal touch, and the cachet of the stranger (*akoma*) in this area, were surely in play.

One of the lessons of this work is that even an insurance plan that is win-win, in which all parties come out ahead, comes face to face with local realities and expectations: different ways to treat health, different ways to manage money, different ways to deal with future uncertainty. Patience is a precious commodity.

Notes

1. First we suggested that when health assistants are recording consultations in the larger ledger, they mark families with insurance separately so they can more easily determine (at year's end) how many consultations were insured. Second, to better calculate the costs and savings of the insurance program, we suggested that the cost of medicine not be recorded at the retail price (as was common practice for many years) but, instead, at the subsidized rate. We also suggested that the differences in pricing for insured families and uninsured families be made more widely known to families at the time of consultation.

References

Bonnal, Jean. n.d. "Republic of Togo." Food and Agricultural Organization of the United Nations, *Online Sourcebook on Decentralization and Local Development*. http://www.ciesin.org/decentralization/English/CaseStudies/TOGO.html.

Ministry of Health, Government of Togo. 2001. "Togo—Health Sector Development—Kara." Report, February 20. http://www-wds.worldbank.org/external/default/WDSContentServer/WDSP/IB/2001/03/09/000094946_01030605394627/Rendered/PDF/multiopage.pdf.

Sala-Diakanda, F., G. Ghesquiere, B. Houinato, and L. P. Tam. 2006. "Community Health Insurance: Assessment and Program Implementation in Rural Togo." Paper presented at the 134th Apha Annual Meeting and Exposition, Boston, November. https://apha.confex.com/apha/134am/techprogram/paper_127490.htm.

6. Youth Migration
Adventure and Suffering
Maria Cecilia Romano

This chapter presents the results of a two-month investigation into youth labor migration in northern Togo, in the village of Farendé. With roots in the country's colonial history, migration for work is not a new phenomenon. What appear to be new are the destinations of young migrants. I tentatively conclude that migration trends, specifically among the Kabre, have evolved from an earlier, cyclical pattern in which people moved mostly between northern and southern Togo. The flow of young laborers now includes increasing international migration to Benin and Nigeria.

Cross-border migration increases the vulnerability of the migrant and is characterized by riskier journeys and placement into more strenuous and dangerous jobs than those of the colonial and early postcolonial practice of working for relatives or acquaintances in southern Togo. Today's young migrants are willing to take these risks and brave potential *souffrances* (suffering) to further their education, support their families, finance apprenticeships and marriages, and quench their thirst for what they refer to as *l'aventure* (adventure).

Village chiefs and elders are quick to characterize this exodus of young people as negative, associating it with greed and with a lust for modernity and "quick money." Many nongovernmental organizations (NGOs) and international organizations similarly denounce the movement of young migrants (especially those younger than eighteen) and label it "child trafficking." Although potentially controversial, I argue that most of these children and youth exhibit extraordinary agency and migrate voluntarily. Their movement cannot be stopped as long as economic insecurity in their communities persists.

The limited resources of both the NGOs working in the area and the Togolese government would be more effective if allocated not toward trying to stop the migration but toward making it safer and its economic returns more reliable. This strategy requires a new, culturally appropriate conceptualization of what "childhood" means for Kabre and of what economic activities are acceptable for children to partake in.

Making youth migration safer is not, of course, a long-term solution. The ultimate goal of the Togolese government and of NGOs that work with this population should be economic growth at the macro level and the expansion of employment opportunities for the communities in question, along with a revamping of the national educational system, for only under these conditions will migrating for employment cease to be so attractive to young people.

Migration in Togo: A History of Movement

Sustained migration patterns in Togo began during the colonial period, as early as 1910, when the Germans discovered that cash crops could not be produced easily in the more arid north. As a result, they turned the northern territories into a labor reserve, recruiting groups such as the Kabre as workers to build the colony's roads in the south and to work in mines (Piot 1999: 40). Young Kabre men, often ten or twenty from each village, left the northern villages each month for southern Togo, where they worked for short stretches of time before returning to the north.

In the 1920s, when the Germans ceded "Togoland" to the French and British, Kabre were again conscripted to work in southern Togo on the colony's roads and railroads, but were now also tasked with bringing under cultivation a fertile but underpopulated area of the south. There they began to produce cash crops such as coffee, cotton, and cocoa for a considerable profit, as the soil was less rocky and more fertile than that in the north. By the mid-1930s, the Kabre began migrating into the southern zone of their own volition, establishing scores of satellite communities. Today more than 200,000 Kabre live and farm in the region (Piot 1999: 42).

Ritual and Diaspora

Despite having relocated, these colonial-era Kabre migrants remained tied to their ancestral villages in the north, returning periodically to sacrifice to spirits and ancestors, to attend funerals, and to initiate their children. Indeed, their continual returns, and the fact that they were wealthier than the northern Kabre, meant that it was largely the money of southerners that financed the ceremonial system in the north, enabling the purchasing of animals and other necessities for ritual. Thus developed an exchange of wealth for ritual, as it were, that has continued to fuel the relationship between north and south.

This north-south relationship is rooted in the Kabre belief that children are dependent on and beholden to their parents, a debt that can never be entirely repaid. Thus, the southerners are regarded as "children" by those in the north. This debt nurtures the expectation that those who have left will send remittances back to the north to replace their lost labor. In principle, "labor flows south—the sons and daughters who depart the north to live and work with family in the south—are replaced by commodity flows north" (Piot 1999: 129). The reality is that the flow of money and commodities such as grain back to the north has been, and continues to be, irregular at best.

The return of southerners to the north is often fraught with tension—with southerners parading their newfound wealth before jealous northerners, and northerners asserting their ritual authority over southern "children." Despite the upper hand of northerners within this system—the fact that "parents" always remain superior to their (southern) children—the allure of southern money and commodities (radios, clothes, bicycles, sometimes cars) has deeply affected those who remain in the north, especially youth. I addressed this in my field notes:

These southern "children" (for example, the family neighboring mine in Farendé, which lives the majority of the year in Togo's southern capital, Lomé) are always welcomed back. It is interesting to see how they quickly readopt or adapt to northern ways and begin to dress, speak, cook, and cultivate as if they lived in the north year-round. When ritual season begins, the ancestral homesteads in the north are flooded with their wealthier southern relatives, and homes are full to the brim with guests and family members sleeping on the floor, some even in the courtyard.

Even so, it is not difficult to identify who is not from Farendé. The southerners I met while living in the village, especially those coming from Lomé, dress very differently. Women wear newer, more colorful, more tailored (and more expensive) pagnes (colorful cloth often wrapped as a skirt) and have more elaborate hairstyles. Men showcase more Western clothing and accessories—dress pants, leather shoes, wristwatches, and briefcases. Often they have motorcycles, sometimes even a car.

The Allure of Modernity

It is this "responsibility to family and homeland on the one hand, and the desire for wealth on the other that has kept Kabre constantly on the move back and forth along the national highway" (Piot 1999: 166). In the same way that the southern diaspora returns to the north, those in the north make periodic trips south.

Some of this occurs during the dry season as people visit family in the south and make extra money working for them. But much of this north-to-south migration occurs as a "mass exodus every July as school children, out for the summer holidays, head south to work for family members and make money to buy books and clothes for school the next year" (Piot 1999: 42). These teens seem to be as at home in the south as in their northern villages, loving the adventure and allure of the modern. Theirs, Piot suggests, is a world in which "sacrifice and MTV, rainmakers and civil servants, fetishists and catechists exist side by side and coauthor an uncontainable hybrid cultural landscape" (Piot 1999: 173). I recorded,

The effects of globalization are felt even here in this small rural village, in a country as "left behind" as Togo. With an increasing number of Internet cafés ("cybers"), both in nearby towns like Kara and now in Farendé itself, young people are being exposed to the Internet, to the wider world, and they crave to be a part of it. This is clearly a significant contributor to youth migration.

Technology is desired and represents a symbol of prestige. People notice whether your Nokia cell phone is in color or not, whether it plays music or not, and which games it has. One of the older boys living in the homestead next door to mine was intrigued with the laptop and solar panel I had brought from the States. He would help me set it up each morning and periodically check to see if all the connections were working properly. I once witnessed him take apart a cell phone and charger because they were not working, bite and twist the frayed wires, connect them to the battery, and charge it in no time. This same young man would then promptly leave all his wires, pick up a handheld hoe, and go cultivate in the fields for hours. Such dichotomies are just part of daily life here.

Another member of my host family was as comfortable using his machete as he was playing with my iPod and Kindle. It was as if he had been around touch-screen technology his whole life. After a day of cultivating, he'd suggest we go to the "movies" and see one of various, fairly recent Hollywood movies or, his personal favorite, a badly dubbed Chinese Kung-Fu film. "Le video" is a bar/boutique in Farendé outfitted with a generator, a 19 [inch] TV, and a DVD player that plays a constant stream of pirated movies from 7 PM to 2 AM. Every weekend night, and most nights when school is out for the summer, it is bursting with young people from the village watching foreign movies, ordering tea and bread, and socializing. For some, this is where plans are made to leave the village and make money elsewhere, and if the intended destination is international—usually Benin or Nigeria, away from kin and family in Togo—the planning at "le video" will be done in secret.

6.1 Farendé teen with color Nokia

Because the cyclical pattern of north-south migration is so ingrained and long-standing within Kabre culture, it is no wonder that the threat of a permanent shift toward migration to Benin and Nigeria is an unhappy one for many of the older generation. Despite the protests of elders, these international destinations hold tremendous allure for the younger generation and struck me as a research topic of importance. In exploring this phenomenon, I aimed to better understand the nature and scale of this historic shift, as well as its social and economic implications.

Methodology

During the two months I spent in Farendé, I completed twenty-eight qualitative interviews with community members—including neighbors, schoolteachers, religious leaders, village chiefs, government volunteers, and government officials. I listened to anyone who wanted to talk about youth migration, but I also set up official interviews through my assistant and translator. We made a conscious effort to choose both men and women of all ages. This came to include young people who had previously migrated, young people who had never migrated but who had friends or siblings who had, and older people with children who may or may not have left the village in search of employment. These interviews typically lasted about an hour and were conducted in French, Kabre, or sometimes a mix of the two. My questions were largely open-ended because I wanted to gain an understanding of the community's experience with and perception of youth migration. When interviewing young Kabre or their parents, my goal was to roughly map the migration history of the household by asking who in the family had migrated and to where, for what kind of work, at what age, for how long, and what the experience was like.

Slowly I started to learn more about the different pathways available to young people who aspire to earn money for themselves and their families; what the process of leaving the village is like; the different types of work young men and women could expect at their destination; the differences among working in southern Togo, Benin, and Nigeria; and, most important, how the community was responding to this phenomenon. While all of these gave me insight into the nature of the shift to international migration that is underway, I felt I needed to complement these qualitative data with quantitative data on the number of young people who are leaving the village each year, exactly where they are traveling to—southern Togo, Benin, or Nigeria—and what they bring back home.

To pursue this more quantitative track, I began by looking at the Farendé medical clinic's latest census records. There are three ledgers, corresponding to each of Farendé three "sectors."[1] I counted how many people in each sector fell into my target population of "youth" from age nine to twenty-five. This range, based on information gathered from my qualitative interviews, represented the ages of young people who were the most likely to migrate. According to the 2011–2012 village census, 767 individuals fell into this range.

I then approached the question of scope in three different ways. First I interviewed all six *chefs du quartier* and asked each of them how many young people had left his (they were all male) *quartier* in the past year and over the previous five years,[2] whether they were mostly male or female, the migrants' average age, the most common destination, and the most common reasons given for leaving the village. This method proved to be too dependent on the chief's mood and memory and did not appear to be statistically accurate.

The second method was to interview the principals, or *directeurs*, of the three village primary schools and the village's combination middle school and high school and ask how many students had dropped out of school during the past year and over the previous five years, how many were boys versus girls, how many of those dropouts were directly linked to the desire to migrate, and of those, where the migrants actually went.

The final method was to go door to door, completing a random sample (about 10 percent) of households in each sector of the village.[3] In each case, I interviewed the head of house about the migration history of his or her family by asking how many people in the household had migrated between age nine and twenty-five during the past year and over the previous five years, where they went, how old they were when they left, and why they decided to leave. This last method was the most painstaking, but it resulted in what seemed to be the most accurate and detailed information. Although the results could certainly be improved by a larger sample size, I learned that roughly 35 percent of young people age nine to twenty-five leave Farendé in search of employment every year; that Benin is the most popular destination; and that the primary motivations are to earn money for one's family and to pay school fees for the coming year.

New Destinations: Stories from Benin and Nigeria

Sweating and slightly out of breath from the soccer match he had just played, the 18-year-old boy sat on a log, accepted a swig of my bottled water and explained to me (in a way that suggested he believed the answer to be self-evident) why young people were leaving the country for work rather than traveling south like before. "There's no money in the south anymore," he said. His two friends and teammates agreed. "Leaving Togo is better. You can make 60,000 CFA [francs]/month ($120) in Benin but only around 30,000 CFA [francs]/month working in the south, which is really too little, even if you don't work on weekends like you do in Benin." When asked about Nigeria, one of these youth replied, "The work there is very hard, but you can return with a motorcycle ('moto') to show family and friends. You might even become a moto-taxi driver and earn more money once back in the village." The youngest of the three boys said that while working in the south is generally safest because you work for family, working in Benin, and Nigeria especially, is simply more profitable and gives one more prestige—"[When you migrate outside of Togo,] you get to see more of the world and might even learn another language. Others come to respect you."

Benin and Nigeria have become the main destinations for young migrant laborers from northern Togo. In fact, during my very first casual conversation about labor migration with young people in Farendé, including neighbors of mine, no one even mentioned southern Togo as a popular place to make money anymore. Perhaps this should not be surprising, as Togo has the lowest gross domestic product per capita of the three countries, at a mere $1,100,[4] but it dramatically disrupts the long-standing Kabre migratory pattern of going to the south of Togo. My young informants had a lot to say about these "new" destinations and the differences between working in each.

First they explained a pervasive stereotype about the kinds of young people who go to each place, saying that youth who "don't do anything" (those who have dropped out of school) go to Nigeria, while "students" go to Benin. When I asked for clarification, they explained that Nigeria is farther away than Benin; thus, the journey to Nigeria is longer, more arduous, and more expensive, typically requiring the help of an intermediary, or *waga*. The wagas make contracts only for a minimum of nine months.[5] Thus, if a school-age teen goes to Nigeria, he will have to skip a year of school. Conversely, interviewees explained that one could work in Benin for as little as two weeks and then return home. This flexibility is what makes Benin such a popular destination for students who mostly want to acquire money for school fees—or, as it is referred to among youth, to *faire la rentrée* (return to school).

Differences between Boys' and Girls' Migration

At first it seemed to me that many more boys were migrating than girls, and while that is the case in the mountain village of Kuwdé, in Farendé boys and girls migrate in close to equal numbers—perhaps with slightly more male migrants. Because of the negative connotations surrounding girls' work, it is not widely spoken about, which makes it seem as if fewer girls leave the village to work in Benin and Nigeria.

The men in this region of northern Togo are some of the best cultivators in the country. Their skills (and cheap labor) are in high demand in Benin and Nigeria, and cultivation is by far the most common form of employment for male migrants, although some may also migrate to begin an apprenticeship in a trade such as carpentry. Since these young men also cultivate for their families and for their community when they are at home in Farendé, this type of work is part of the landscape, part of their history,

6.2 Boys cultivating.

and part of village culture. Thus, the work they do abroad is frequently discussed as they and their elders compare soil conditions, techniques, and tools abroad with those of Farendé.

By contrast, girls end up working either in bars or in households as domestic servants, with the majority (roughly 60 percent) ending up in bars, a job that does not exist for young women in Farendé. There are other possibilities, such as working as a phone booth operator or working at a *boutique*,[6] but often these migrant women have no say in their work placement, especially if they have a "bad" or self-interested waga who only wants to make money off them.

Working as a barmaid often turns into sex work after hours. A girl's employer can threaten to kick her out if she does not sleep with him or his customers. In Nigeria, this would mean being alone in an unfamiliar country, facing a language barrier, and having no means of returning home, so most have little choice. The sad truth about sex labor is that it is heavily stigmatized in Togo, which means that few girls are comfortable talking about their experiences, especially since some are rumored to have been infected with HIV/AIDS while abroad, while others have brought back unwanted pregnancies.

Boys are most likely to work on family-owned farms in Benin and Nigeria. In Benin, these are sometimes the farms of Kabre who have moved there. In Nigeria, they are most often the farms of Muslim Yoruba, who are said to be the wealthiest community there. In both places, young men are typically recruited to work in groups and are paid at the end of each month (in Benin) or at the end of the year (in Nigeria).

Girls are more likely to work spread out in different bars or houses, even if they are recruited together. Work conditions in homes are not typically dangerous, but the girls may experience verbal or physical abuse and almost always work unfairly long hours. The labor is also very arduous: they cook for all members of the family, clean, tend to children, run errands, and more, as shown by the following testimony of a girl I interviewed:

I knew a girl who had gone to Benin before me. She was a classmate of mine. She dropped out of school at age 17 because she had recently lost both of her parents and needed to make money to support herself. Her plan was to earn enough to start an apprenticeship in tailoring. She came back to Farendé a year ago and told me that it is

6.3 Girls returned from Benin.

very hard work over there, but that she had to endure and earn. She went back to Benin shortly afterward.

A year ago when I was 16 my father passed away and I too decided to go to Benin to make money to keep my little brother and sister in school. I was approached by a "grande soeur" who knew of a family who needed a domestic worker in their home.[7] I agreed to go with her. My wage had already been negotiated. My grande soeur paid for the transportation and told me there would be another girl traveling with us. She was 17 and was going to sell food in small restaurants and by the side of the road, but she ended up working in a different city than me, so I don't know much else about her experience.

I worked in the home of a married couple, both civil servants, with two young children. From 5 AM to 9 AM my responsibilities were to do the dishes, sweep, prepare breakfast for the parents before they went to work, and bathe and feed the children before school. At noon I would bring the kids back from school and make them lunch. At 2 PM I would take the children back to school and finally bring them back to the home at 5 PM at the end of their day. Supper was to be ready every day by 6 PM, and I never went to sleep before 10 PM. I was paid 10,000 CFA [francs]/month (about $20). Though I ate the leftovers of the food I prepared for the family at no deduction to my salary, I did have to spend what I earned on toiletries, clothes, and other necessities. As often as I could, I sent back money and notebooks to my siblings and mother in Farendé with people I knew who were passing through Benin.

After a year I decided to return to Farendé because the work was tiresome and I was not being paid enough. I suspect my grande soeur was taking an advance on my salary that she never informed me about. I could have stayed longer. The family was pleased with my work, but I don't think I could have renegotiated a better salary. Now I would like to return to school.

When I asked this young woman what she would tell younger girls who were thinking about migrating to Benin, she said she would advise them to negotiate a good wage with the grande soeur beforehand and to make sure she is trustworthy.

In bars the work is more dangerous, but the hours are often shorter, depending on the informal sex work done after hours. Bars can also be more profitable because sex work adds "tips" to a salary that is already comparable to that of domestic labor. Girls predominantly go to Benin, although some go to Nigeria. Girls in both Benin and Nigeria are paid in cash each month, but they may also bring back pagnes (cloth), dishware, or other household goods. A girl working in a home might receive 10,000–20,000 CFA francs ($20–$40) a month, while a girl working in a bar will receive about 15,000 CFA francs plus tips.

On Wagas and Vulnerability

Although international migration outside kinship networks is inherently more risky than migration to southern Togo, Benin is regarded by most as "safer" than Nigeria for four reasons. First, as previously stated, it is closer to Togo,[8] so the journey is shorter, less expensive, and one is less likely to encounter mishaps. Second, there are pockets of Kabre in Benin, so the young migrants often share a language and culture (not to mention currency, as Benin also uses the CFA franc) with the people they end up working for, even if they are not relatives or acquaintances, as they might have been in southern Togo. In Nigeria, by contrast, there are enormous differences in culture, religion, and language, making it very hard to fend for oneself and find one's way home should a migrant suffering from abuse or exploitation want to leave his place of employment. Third, young labor migrants who go to Benin are most often paid in cash, whereas those who go to Nigeria are paid in goods or commodities, such as motorcycles, sound systems, tin for the roof of a homestead, and other objects of social prestige, when their contract is up. When one is paid in objects rather than money, one risks being cheated because the item could be of poor quality or simply worth less than the labor one put in for the contracted amount of time. Further, it is not unheard of, for young men especially, to go for a year or sometimes more working tirelessly for a waga and an employer, only to be told at the conclusion of his contract that there will be no payment. With no bargaining power, there is little a migrant can do in this situation other than find a way to return home empty-handed. Fourth and most important, the short distance and the fact that Benin is the most popular destination from Farendé means that there is more information and awareness about conditions there versus those in Nigeria, and more people, including one's family and friends, are able to give one advice about where to go and what kinds of jobs to avoid. Migrants to Benin are less dependent, in general, on wagas.

Wagas are typically responsible for the migrant's transportation to the place where he or she will work, for securing employment, and for collecting and transferring payment to the migrant from the employer when the time is up. Wagas can merely be good friends who "know the way" and who have been to Benin or Nigeria once or several times before, or they can be recruiters, in a sense, on behalf of employers in Benin or Nigeria.

As I was finishing up my interviews at the end of the two months, a trend concerning wagas became very clear to me. The more personally a migrant knew his or her waga, the less likely he or she was to be cheated or led into harm's way. Youth who were wooed by an unfamiliar waga who had perhaps come into Farendé on a motorcycle, wearing fine clothes, and promising to help get them anything they wanted if they left in secret to work abroad, were typically the ones who ended up with exploitative employers, while the waga ended up pocketing the contract wages and disappearing. Youth who left for Benin or Nigeria with a friend who had been there before typically ended up working for employers who were known to be kind and fair, and they usually had positive experiences.

Persisting Motivations for Migration and the Allure of *l'Aventure*

Given the uncertainty, the potential for exploitation, and the risk of having to return empty-handed, why do these young men and women continue to leave their village—one of subsistence but not extreme poverty—to work in Benin and Nigeria? Obviously, each migrant has his or her own story, his or her own motivation for embarking on this particular journey (sometimes many times over), but there are a few very common rationalizations.

The two reasons that I heard most often from migrants themselves were related to providing for family and coping with the public education system. Often a parent falls ill, and in a society where large families with many children are still the norm—each family has many mouths to feed—older children may be called on to help. As there are few employment opportunities near the village, they travel abroad where they imagine (because they have heard the rumors) that money is waiting for them. Wagas who recruit young labor often target families in dire situations, for youth in such families may be hard-pressed to decline the promise of a job and a quick end to their financial insecurity.

The second most common narrative is related to the inadequacies of the rural educational system. Full classrooms and a lack of trained teachers make for a tough learning environment for anyone, but especially for children who cannot afford kerosene to fill their lanterns to do their homework at night, who may not have enough to eat, or who must cultivate and do other laborious chores when they return from school each day. This causes many to fail their exams, and after a while they get discouraged or their parents decide it is not worth the money to send the child to school anymore (especially if the child in question is a girl). In fact, school fees rose in 1998, and all students were suddenly responsible for buying their own uniforms, shoes, notebooks, and pens. An interview with a village schoolteacher also revealed that secondary school students in Farendé must pay 10,000 CFA francs/year ($20) in tuition and roughly 5,000 CFA francs more for books and other supplies. Those children whose families cannot afford this must either migrate for a short time to earn the fees or ultimately drop out. Many older siblings end up migrating to support their younger siblings' continued education through remittances.[9]

All of these pressing reasons for migrating made perfect sense to me, but I still struggled to understand why some young people chose Nigeria over Benin as a destination. Even though Nigeria is known for being where work is hardest and most exploitative, especially for boys, young men choose Benin and Nigeria as their destination in almost equal numbers. In Benin, the family you work for houses and feeds you with no deduction to your pay, but in Nigeria you are often expected to construct your own shelter and prepare your own food, even after a long day of hard labor. I also found out from a former migrant-turned-waga that in Nigeria one is sometimes exposed to work-enhancing drugs that are put into young migrants' food without their knowledge.

As if the advantages of migrating to Benin over Nigeria did not seem obvious enough, let me add another point of comparison: the way young male migrants are paid in the two countries. In Benin, one is paid for each task completed, such as weeding, planting, cultivating, or harvesting, usually by the quarter-hectare (un carré). One young migrant who had been to southern Togo, Benin, and Nigeria multiple times told me that cultivating un carré in southern Togo would earn 6,000 CFA francs ($12), whereas in Benin it would earn 7,000 CFA francs—or 7,500 CFA francs "if it had tall grass." In Nigeria, however, it is more common to be under contract with a waga, so one is paid at the end of the year with whatever item the migrant chose at the onset. Most migrants said that if they added up the number of carrés they had cultivated in Nigeria—and been paid the going rate in Benin—they would have received far more than the monetary value of a motorcycle or whatever item had been promised in their contract.

I was told by a young man who used to be a waga that six months of hard labor in Nigeria usually earned a male migrant a motorcycle (worth about 300,000 CFA francs, or $600). Nine months is worth a motorcycle plus some money or a sound system or tin for a roof. One year is equal to a motorcycle plus more money plus a sound system or tin. If one factors in that these young men typically cultivate seven days a week, and cultivate a quarter-hectare per day, just six months in Nigeria at the going rate in Benin (7,000 CFA francs per day) would earn them more than a million CFA francs, three to four times the value of a motorcycle.

"When older boys come back from Nigeria on their motorcycles, their younger siblings and neighbors see only the cool new vehicle, not the suffering the boy endured. When the boy no longer has money for gasoline, he will sell the motorcycle for a third of its value and, penniless as before, will return to Nigeria for another round of work. They are addicted to the adventure," one father said during an interview.

If the items earned are clearly not worth the back-breaking labor in Nigeria, why do young men still sometimes choose Nigeria over Benin? I found three reasons. First, a young man in Farendé who urgently needs to earn money cannot be too careful with opportunities that might pass him by, so if a waga tells him he will take him to Nigeria, he might simply go rather than weighing his options. Second, the realities of life in Nigeria for young migrants are not often discussed in the village. The fact that young men and women leave their homes in the middle of the night to meet their wagas and depart, often without informing their parents, only adds to the mystique. Third, and most important, there is the element of what the Farendé

6.4 Nigerian motorcycle.

father referred to as "adventure." Although this is not necessarily rational from an economic standpoint, it is "cooler" to arrive in Farendé astride a new motorcycle than with money that one would then be pressured to save or spend on family. The allure of the Nigerian adventure is the allure of the modern, of technology, of life outside the small village these youth call home. Leaving for Nigeria carries the connotation that one will see the world, learn new languages, experience different cultures—and, perhaps, touch modernity if they work in a large town or city. Ultimately, many young migrants choose Nigeria despite its risks and reputation because it is more of an adventure.

Perceptions of Youth Migration

One question I struggled with the entire time I was in Togo was whether youth labor migration was "good" or "bad." On the one hand, the employment of young people, especially employment abroad where jobs pay better than in southern Togo, is allowing some to continue their education, to care for their families, to finance apprenticeships, and to build their futures back home in the village. Yet the older generations, village authority figures, and heads of NGOs I interviewed seemed uniformly against young people leaving the village for work.

Parents I interviewed protested that this younger generation cared only about making quick money and buying motorcycles, cell phones, new sound systems, and other flashy things. Fearing the unknown and fearing for the safety of their children abroad, they asserted that it would be better for them to stay and cultivate in Farendé or to make money in nearby Ketao or Kara. "Even though it is not as much as one could make in Benin or Nigeria, it is enough to pay school fees," one mother said. Even so, another parent conceded that employment nearby is hard to come by, so if one can earn more abroad and if a child's education depends on this money, it is hard to deny him or her the opportunity. Still another regretted that he had no say at all in his son's future, as he left for Nigeria in the middle of the night without informing him, and was staunchly against all young people who "abandoned their families" to work abroad.

When I interviewed the village chief of Farendé, he began by criticizing how the government and the village's wealthy "children" in the south (not only cash-cropping cultivators but also civil servants) had not invested sufficiently in Farendé's well-being and development, but he also blamed the youth for foolishly leaving to chase the illusion of "adventure." He said that more often than not they returned empty-handed to a village that is less able to feed them than it was when they left (because their families had lost their labor in the interim). The French sociologist Yves Marguerat holds a similar view, arguing that the migration of youth has a crippling effect on the departure zones. Not only are these areas losing a young and vibrant labor force, he says, but they are also losing those who have the capacity for innovation, those who will improvise and try out new agricultural techniques (Marguerat 1994: 254).

I must say that, in the case of Farendé, youth do not entirely abandon their village. Most young migrants do return from Benin and Nigeria, and, unlike earlier patterns of migration to southern Togo, settle down and have families back home. One young migrant in particular stands out in my mind. Twenty-nine years old at the time of our interview, he had been to the south of Togo four times, to Benin more than three times, and to Nigeria twice for work. He fully subscribed to the idea that "to earn, one must suffer." And earn he did. In fact, he earned enough to start an apprenticeship as a carpenter and then saved enough money to build himself a home in Farendé. In his case, it was a labor of love in that he did it to accumulate bride wealth and win the hand of the woman who is now his wife. He told us that many young men go through this. "Maybe you want to construct a house here in the village but your family has no money, maybe you need to take care of aging parents," he said. "There are many reasons to leave to earn money."

After hearing his story, I thought back to our drive up to Farendé from the capital at the very beginning of the summer:

As our group was traveling the seven hours to the north from Lomé, I couldn't help but notice the many empty houses on either side of the rutted, bumpy road. They weren't old and worn, however, just unfinished. Once we got to the village and moved in with our host families, I noticed that some of my would-be neighbors were actually similar, sprawling yet incomplete homesteads. Where were the owners?

It suddenly dawned on me that maybe these unfinished homes were those of young migrants who were steadily sending money and building materials back to their villages, slowly building new homes. When migration was mostly to the south, many would end up settling there, but since migration abroad is outside the Kabre kinship network, these migrants have no way to fully entrench themselves at these destinations. In theory, they now come back with more money, with the intent to settle in the village, and, in this young man's case, with new skills with which to advance village life, however slightly.

Organizations such as Togo's branch of CARE International, Human Rights Watch, and local development agencies such as Farendé's Actions Sociales see youth migration in a different light. Since some of the migrants are younger than eighteen and thus considered "children" according to the United Nations Convention on the Rights of the Child, their "acquisition and movement by improper means such as force, fraud or deception" (regardless of whether the child "consented," as long as the child's acquisition is for exploitation) is regarded as "trafficking" (Hashim and Thorsen 2011: 17). I suggest, however, that this distinction between what does and does not constitute trafficking is largely unhelpful. Trafficking by force for the purpose of exploitation is easy to label as bad and illegal, but when the lines are blurred, when intermediaries or traffickers themselves are underage, when migrants are fully willing, and when the outcomes of autonomous child migration are positive, what are we to call it?

The question of whether this labor migration is good or bad gets even trickier when the young migrants themselves have differing opinions about their individual experiences. Some fifteen-year-olds are delighted that they were able to go to Benin and earn their own spending money for school fees and new clothes. Others are resentful that they left for Nigeria, were cheated out of motorcycles, and lost a year of schooling.

I tend to agree with Ann Whitehead of the Development Research Center on Migration Globalization and Poverty (DRC); Charlotte Min-Harris, the author of "Youth Migration and Poverty in Sub-Saharan Africa: Empowering the Rural Youth"; and other academics, such as Iman Hashim and Dorte Thorsen (2011), who argue that the discourse that surrounds child trafficking robs young migrants of the agency they display when they make the decision to leave the village to earn money.[10] Their thirst for adventure, their hopefulness, and their desire for a life beyond mere subsistence has the potential to be a driving force of development for villages such as Farendé—which still lacks electricity and running water—as long as steps are taken to prevent the more negative aspects of youth migration.

Conclusion

I acknowledge that misfortunes may arise from the vulnerability inherent in the international migration of youth, especially of those younger than eighteen, but I believe that exploitation at the hands of employers and self-interested wagas can be prevented if the community works together. First, there needs to be open discussion about youth migration and its repercussions. The current silence around the topic, especially for young girls, only adds to the allure. Young people who successfully earn money from kind employers and with the help of "good" intermediaries should share their stories and their contacts so that other aspiring young migrants can follow in their footsteps and have similarly positive experiences. Likewise, those migrants who suffer abuse or who are cheated out of their pay must advise would-be migrants against certain wagas and employers and even against entire occupations or destinations. A lot can be accomplished through peer education.

With open communication, young people will be better informed not only of the dangers they might face, but also of what constitutes a fair salary for different types of work, and as such will have more bargaining power when approached by wagas in the future. Instead of taking the first offer that comes to them, they will know to negotiate (possibly even with the help of their parents or village elders) a fair wage, safe passage, and placement with reputable employers before departing. If this openness comes to fruition, more young migrants will have positive experiences and will be able to contribute more money and potentially new skills to their communities.

This strategy requires a new conceptualization of childhood, for the cutoff age of eighteen in the official definition of trafficking ignores the realities of childhood in a place like Togo, where children often "come of age" and begin providing for families long before then.[11] Further, many children in Farendé are not even sure of their true ages, because their parents never acquired birth certificates when they were born. The DRC's studies on autonomous child migration, which have been conducted in India, Ghana, Burkina Faso, and Bangladesh, find that "high rates of child migration occur from relatively impoverished areas where many adults use migration as part of survival or livelihood strategies. . . . In these circumstances many children migrate to meet their own ambitions and aspirations, or out of their own sense of responsibility to their parents. They are certainly not simply pawns in family livelihood strategies, nor are they the victims of traffickers."[12] I find this to be the case for most young migrants I encountered in Farendé.

Regarding children as exercising agency in their decisions to migrate and acknowledging that these journeys may hold positive outcomes is controversial, for it challenges our prevailing conceptions of childhood.[13] Further, we need to acknowledge that viewing children as agentive can be problematic in the context of policy making, for the government has a responsibility to put a stop to the more egregious cases of forced migration and exploitation at the hands of intermediaries (such as those that have indeed been seen in Togo).[14] Nongovernmental organizations especially cannot risk being seen as facilitating child labor, but denouncing youth migration as "child trafficking" and seeing it as illegal plunges the phenomenon further into secrecy, making it even more dangerous.

These lawmaking and advocacy organizations should actively work toward making youth migration safer and more successful by encouraging open community discussion and peer education. Further supporting this view is the fact that current efforts to stop youth migration have been largely unsuccessful. One of my host brothers told me that young students can simply flash their school IDs at the Benin border control station. Apparently, the gendarmes know that young Togolese kids often go to Benin to earn money for school, so they allow them to pass. If they or their wagas encounter any problems, it takes but a simple bribe to convince these officials to let them through. If they continue to encounter difficulties in crossing, they either try another time or cross elsewhere, on a bush path. I strongly believe that neither laws and regulations nor border patrol can stop a young person who truly wants to experience l'aventure or whose family is in desperate need of money. The only way this phenomenon might stop is if there is economic growth at the macro level and if Togo's education system is dramatically improved. In the meantime, as long as negative experiences are prevented, youth migration has the potential to provide temporary relief from poverty or a way for students to stay in school.

Making youth migration safer and more successful is not a long-term solution. Ultimately, interested organizations and the Togolese government should work to bring subsidies back to rural schooling, including the purchasing of "kits scolaires," which include uniforms and school supplies at no cost to the recipient, and to make the schools capable of retaining students by adding high-quality teachers and improving learning outcomes. For education to be an incentive to stay in the village, children need to be able to see its tangible economic returns. For that reason, the government must also work to expand employment opportunities for educated youth, not only though gardening for young men and animal raising for young women (both of which require access to land, fertilizers, water pumps, loans, and electricity),[15] but also through advanced agricultural technology and other jobs that advance the development of these rural communities.

In this setting where school is too expensive for many families and where there are far too few viable employment options for rural youth, youth migration should be made safer rather than condemned so young people and their families can enjoy its positive outcomes.[16] Further research should look at exactly how viable this migration can be, under the right circumstances, to a household's accumulation strategy and how remittances affect home communities, as well as individual families' standard of living.

Notes

1. Farendé has three sectors: the area on the mountain, called Farendé Montagne or, in Kabre, Farang Poɣo; the area in the plain north of the main road, called Farendé Plaine Nord; and the area in the plain south of the main road, called Farendé Plaine Sud. This was the current method of dividing the village as explained to me by the head of the village clinic.
2. The village is also divided into six *quartiers*, each of which has a chief. As these chiefs have intimate knowledge of the families in their quartiers, I sought them out to ask how many young people had been leaving the village for work.
3. The number of households in each sector also came from the 2011 village census.
4. The CIA World Factbook in 2012 estimated Benin's per capita gross domestic product at $1,700 and Nigeria's as $2,700. Central Intelligence Agency, Africa, Benin. https://www.cia.gov/library/publications/the-world-factbook/geos/bn.html. Accessed December 20, 2015. Central Intelligence Agency, Africa, Nigeria. https://www.cia.gov/library/publications/the-world-factbook/geos/ni.html. Accessed December 20, 2015.
5. Agreements made with wagas are oral contracts and typically delineate how long a migrant will work (nine months, a year, two years, etc.) and what form his or her compensation will take (a motorcycle, a sound system, tin for roofs, or money). As explained in the next section, compensation for work in Nigeria, especially for boys, typically takes the form of *things*, not cash.

6. Boutiques sell food and supplies but do not serve alcohol.
7. Grande soeur literally means "elder sister" but typically refers to a female waga who is not related to the migrant.
8. The border is only 18 kilometers from Farendé, following the road to Ketao and to the official border crossing station, and about 12 kilometers if one takes a direct route on foot to avoid the border authorities, as many migrants do.
9. A child who drops out of school may also decide that he or she wants to do an apprenticeship to be a seamstress or a carpenter, but financing this training, which lasts several years and is unpaid, can cost exorbitant sums of money.
10. Other scholars who have contributed to or are frequently cited as part of this ongoing discussion are Ariès 1962; Archer 1988; Chandra 2008; Huijsmans 2012.
11. Coomer and Hubbard (2009) present an interesting study of age, labor, and childhood in Namibia.
12. "DRC Migration, Globalisation and Poverty," 2003, http://www.migrationdrc.org.
13. There is a growing body of literature that discusses children and agency in this context: see Ansell 2005; Bluebond-Langner and Korbin 2007; Ennew et al. 2005; Klocker 2007.
14. Amanda Day and Joseph Struble, with CARE Togo, "Togo Child Trafficking Stories," 2005. CARE Togo. http://youthcentertogo.org/doc/TogoStories.pdf.
15. Gardening in this area typically involves growing peppers, tomatoes, and onions, which can be sold in local markets at considerable profit.
16. For discussions of child labor and migration in Africa, see Awumbila and Whitehead 2009 for West Africa generally; Dougnon 2011 for Mali; Klocker 2007 and May 2003 for Tanzania. For other areas of the world, see Campoamor 2012 for Peru; Chandra 2008, Dube 1981, and Rajan 2013 for India; and Huijsmans 2008 and Huijsmans and Baker 2012 for Thailand.

References

Ariès, Philippe. 1962. *Centuries of Childhood: A Social History of Family Life*. New York: Alfred A. Knopf.
Ansell, Nicola. 2005. *Children, Youth, and Development*. London: Routledge.
Archer, Margaret Scotford. 1988. *Culture and Agency: The Place of Culture in Social Theory*. Cambridge: Cambridge University Press.
Awumbila, Mariama, and Ann Whitehead. 2009. "Proceedings of Child and Youth Migration in West Africa: Research Progress and Implications for Policy." University of Ghana, Accra. http://www.migrationdrc.org/news/reports/Child_and _Youth_Migration/Child%20and%20Youth%20Migration%20in%20West%20 Africa%20conference%20report.pdf.
Bluebond-Langner, Myra, and Jill E. Korbin. 2007. "Challenges and Opportunities in the Anthropology of Childhoods: An Introduction to Children, Childhoods, and Childhood Studies?" *American Anthropologist* 109, no. 2: 241–46.

Campoamor, Leigh. 2012. "Public Childhoods: Street Labor, Family, and the Politics of Progress in Peru." PhD diss., Duke University, Durham, NC.

Chandra, Vinod. 2008. *Children's Domestic Work: Children Speak out for Themselves.* Delhi, India: Manak.

Coomer, Rachel, and Diane Hubbard. 2009. "A Major Decision: Considering the Age of Majority in Namibia." In *Children's Rights in Namibia*, ed. Oliver Christian Ruppel, 101–20. Windhoek: Macmillan Education Namibia.

Dougnon, Isaie. 2011. "Child Trafficking or Labor Migration? A Historical Perspective from Mali's Dogon Country." *Humanity* 2, no. 1. http://www.humanityjournal .org/humanity-volume-2-issue-1/child-trafficking-or-labor-migration-historical -perspective-malis-dogon-co.

Dube, Leela. 1981. "The Economic Roles of Children in India: Methodological Issues." In *Child Work, Poverty, and Underdevelopment*, ed. Gerry Rodgers and Guy Standing, 179–213. Geneva: International Labour Office.

Ennew, Judith, William. E. Myers, and Dominique P. Plateau. 2005. "Defining Child Labor as if Human Rights Really Matter." In *Child Labor and Human Rights: Making Children Matter*, ed. Burns H. Weston. Boulder, CO: Lynne Rienner.

Hashim, Iman, and Dorte Thorsen. 2011. *Child Migration in Africa.* London: Zed.

Huijsmans, Roy. 2008. "Children Working beyond Their Localities: Lao Children Working in Thailand." *Childhood* 15, no. 3: 331–53.

Huijsmans, Roy, and Simon Baker. 2012. "Child Trafficking: 'Worst Form' of Child Labour, or Worst Approach to Young Migrants?" *Development and Change* 43, no. 4: 919–46.

Klocker, Natascha. 2007. "An Example of Thin Agency: Child Domestic Workers in Tanzania." In *Global Perspectives on Rural Childhood and Youth: Young Rural Lives*, ed. Ruth Panelli, Samantha Punch, and Elsbeth Robson. New York: Routledge.

Marguerat, Yves. 1994. *Population, migrations, urbanisation au Togo et en Afrique Noire: Articles et documents (1981–1993).* Lomé, Togo: Presses de l'Université du Bénin.

May, Ann. 2003. "Unexpected Migrations: Urban Labor Migration of Rural Youth and Maasai Pastoralists in Tanzania" PhD diss., University of Colorado, Boulder.

Piot, Charles. 1999. *Remotely Global: Village Modernity in West Africa.* Chicago: University of Chicago Press.

Rajan, Sebastian I. 2013. "Internal Migration and Youth in India: Main Features, Trends and Emerging Challenges." Report, Centre for Development Studies, Kerala, India.

7. Cyber Village
Connor Cotton

I wake up from a night of confused dreams, brought on by the constant heat and the stress that has been building since I arrived, looking around a room that I still feel unfamiliar with. After I get up off the straw mattress and try to stretch out some of the stiffness I feel, I get dressed enough to open the door and retrieve the hot water my host family leaves for me just outside the threshold every morning—no hint as to which person brought it or how long ago that person woke up to make sure it was there when I opened the door. I will never get used to this kind of hospitality.

After a breakfast made from groceries purchased once a week from a shopping expedition into the regional capital, I make my way to the shower. Really it's just a brick stall with a corrugated metal door that has long since fallen off its hinges and now has to be leaned against the opening to offer any privacy. Early in the morning, doused with fresh water from the well, is the only time I feel cool.

That is about as far as a description of my "typical day" can go. I spent eight weeks in Togo, and each one was radically different from the one before it. When I designed my project, I had a rosy vision of myself having weeks to carefully design, construct, and establish a computer center before my time was up. I thought my days would be spent largely in the building that would house the materials I had been reviewing for weeks, spending this many days on surveying, that many days on design. If only . . .

While my partner, another Duke student, and I had raised enough money for everything we needed for the computer center before we left, that money was in an account with thousands of other dollars destined for other programs at Duke. Before we could access it, it would need to be transferred to the Trinity School fund; then we would need to wait for it to be transferred to the cultural anthropology account; then we would need to wait until it was processed into our professor's research account. In all, we would have to wait six weeks from our arrival in Togo for our materials to arrive—and almost seven for them to become available.

My time before the materials arrived was spent *trying* to be useful. To understand why this was so hard, I need to explain something that I struggled with the entirety of my experience: I have never taken a French class—or any class on a spoken language, for that matter. I have never been outside the English-speaking world. I have never taken a class in cultural anthropology, sociology, global health, or psychology.

At this point, you may be asking why I ever thought it was a good idea to go to a Francophone West African country under the direction of a professor of cultural anthropology along with six global health students. If you are, then you are asking yourself the same question I was tortured with whenever I looked into the face of someone with whom I had almost no means of relating to or communicating.

What I *have* done is build robots. I have taken classes in structural engineering. I have stood in ninety-degree heat and taught high school students who have never picked up a hammer to build a deck and wheelchair ramp in three days. But most important, I have listened to someone tell me that she wanted to build a solar-powered, Internet-connected computer center in the middle of an off-grid Togolese village and decided that she would have a better chance of accomplishing that goal with me than without me.

But as I walked through the local market, totally helpless if anyone deviated from the minuscule amount of French I had managed to learn, I wondered whether I could have done a better job of preparing. Could I have spent less time reviewing the electrical array and more time with Rosetta Stone software learning French? Could I have read less about the components before selecting them and more about this society's culture? Or, most damning of all—could I have spent less time on Facebook and Hulu and more time on something that actually mattered?

This was one part of my mind-set before the materials arrived.

Every major attempt at development in this area has failed. That was the other part. Our professor had given us a small history of the community we would be living with for two months before we arrived. The takeaway lesson from the story is that many well-intentioned charitable groups have come to Farendé over the past few decades, and none of them has been successful at accomplishing what it intended.

I am a twenty-year-old college student who has trouble waking up in time for his 10:05 class. Organizations with tens of thousands of dollars at their disposal, people with years of experience and prestigious degrees behind them, all with much more time than I had, have tried to implement their programs. They have all failed. What am I expecting to do?

"I BELIEVE!! I BELIEVE IN FARENDÉ!" shouts Elie as he stands up from the table. We had spent the day attempting to negotiate with an Internet provider who was refusing to install a prearranged system until I paid the technician a bribe. As a break from the frustration, Elie, our local contact, had suggested we get lunch and then a drink with his best friend to see if he had a suggestion.

Days earlier, two other Duke students had met with the préfet (district administrator) of the region that encompassed Farendé. He told them that he had just signed the paperwork to bring electricity to the village that has been waiting for the utility for years, long after surrounding villages were provided access. When would the work begin? "Soon." But estimates for extending the existing power grid to the village were upward of $500,000.

I had just finished explaining an alternative plan. Instead of building additional power-generating capacity into currently existing plants and then paying for transformers to compensate for the transmission loss over the distance to Farendé, why not build small-scale solar power installations inside the village? Over short distances, transformers would not be necessary. Far fewer power lines would have to be erected. Programs and pricing could be set in place to incentivize use during hours of peak use and decrease the need for batteries. The increase in price from using solar instead of traditional power generators would be more than balanced by these decreases. The best part is, in the long run, electricity would be cheaper in Farendé than anywhere else in Togo.

Elie's community has been neglected and deceived by its government. It has been given almost nothing but false hope from nongovernmental organizations (NGOs) proclaiming themselves saviors. It has been losing its youth to a stream of migration because the young people have lost hope in the community's way of life. Yet Elie still works to bring progress.

Why? Although the odds may be stacked against him, there is still a chance for success, and that chance is worth fighting for. I was already in Farendé. What I could or should have done while I was back in America had become irrelevant for the time being. Even if I would only have days for a project I thought would take weeks, even if I was sick, and even if I was struggling with the social and linguistic barriers of my host community, I still had my own chance at success. What I learned from Elie was to keep fighting.

I sit on the couch in my living room talking to my parents as muted television commercials play in the background. My mom has just finished reading *The Boy Who Harnessed the Wind*, the story of a boy from rural Zimbabwe who constructed an electricity-generating windmill from pictures he found in a physics textbook at his village's library. "If one boy could do that with access to a book, think of what an entire village of children could do with access to the Internet!" she says excitedly. "I know!" I say. "That's the whole point of the project. People there will teach themselves how to do things instead of needing to stay reliant on outsiders to do things for them." Finally, my parents are beginning to understand the reasoning behind my project of building an Internet café in the village of Farendé in northern Togo. Not only that, but they seem to be excited about it rather than dreading my departure for West Africa the next day.

"This is going to change everything. They'll be able to build irrigation systems, better roads, get better health care, better education . . . better lives!" says my dad. "Exactly," I reply, smiling. This is going to change everything.

I struggled to breathe as my mother held me as tight she could. She burst into tears as she dropped me off at the airport, telling me as I lugged my duffel bag full of tools and medical supplies over the curb, "Just, please, come back alive." The luggage attendant who was coming forward to help me with my bags laughed cheerfully, trying to reassure her. "He'll be back safe and sound! No worries, ma'am!" Once her SUV had pulled away and we were inside the terminal, he started to speak in a slight accent that suggested he was from somewhere in Anglophone West Africa. "So, where are you off to?" he asked. "Northern Togo," I said, unsure whether he would recognize the name of a country I had not heard of until a year ago. "I'm doing a construction project in a village there." Suddenly his face changed, the pleasant smile replaced by an enigmatic and inquisitive gaze as he turned to look at me. "Have you ever been to Africa before?" he asked. "No, sir," I responded, getting the same feeling that came into my stomach when I had talked to the sales attendant at the electrical supply store who refused to sell me the parts I needed because he did not believe I was qualified for the project. "Well," he said as he hoisted my bags onto the check-in counter, "just come back alive, OK?" He clapped me on the shoulder, shook my hand, and turned to the woman behind the counter: "This boy is going to Africa!"

That's all I am—a boy.

Someone looking at me might have thought I was fifteen. In reality, I was twenty years old. The difference did not really seem to matter. I still felt like someone who was too young to be trying what I was aiming to do.

The man in the white lab coat eyes my passport suspiciously. I had tried to look confident as I handed it to him, praying he would wave me through without checking for the yellow booklet listing my vaccinations. *How could I have forgotten to put it there? I think. I stayed up all night and forgot to do one of the only things I needed to do! What else have I forgotten?*

Others who do not have the necessary proof of their yellow fever vaccination are being sent into a room off to the side, presumably to receive the shot. I was not relishing the idea of getting an injection in a high-volume clinic that I, arrogantly or not, judged to be below U.S. standards of hygiene. The man did exactly what I was dreading and looked for the form. When it was not there, he began asking questions—questions I had no way to understand, because I did not speak French. *Wait, people in the airport don't even speak English? I'm already screwed. Why didn't I learn more French?!*

Thankfully, Cheyenne, one of the two other Duke students I am traveling with, steps forward and intervenes by translating for me. I tell the man that I was vaccinated for yellow fever but packed the form in one of my checked bags. Baggage claim is behind him, so he will have to let me pass in order to get it. Then I will come back and show it to him. He agrees to let me through. Once Ben, the last student we are traveling with, Cheyenne, and I have our bags, we make our way through customs and toward the area where we will wait for our faculty mentor and his assistant to pick us up. *I hope I don't need my proof of vaccination to get out*, I think, knowing full well that in reality it has never been in my bags. It is on the kitchen table in Virginia. Things are off to a great start.

The man at the front of the bus continues his rant—onto another list of benefits his tonic will give anyone who buys it from him. "Strength! Beauty! Youth! All can be yours . . . for a small fee!" Parts of his speech are in French; others are in Kabre and Ewe. Just as I have given up all hope of getting any sleep on the trip from Lomé, Togo's capital, to the capital of the region where the project will take place, he starts yelling in English: "I do not make this! The white man makes this!" Later, as he walks down the aisle to collect money, he nods to me and says, *"Yovo"*—Ewe for "white person."

Time seems to have been racing by since we arrived in the north. My partner and I have spent only one day with our host family, but I am eager to get started on work, so today we have hiked up the mountain to Kuwdé to meet with our professor at the Case de Santé (Health Hut), a community clinic that is many people's only access to biomedical care. We have just finished a tour of the facility, and Basile, the health worker who runs the clinic, has asked whether I would be able to renovate the hot water system. *You've never done plumbing before. You've never done official plumbing before. You've put pipes together. You wouldn't know what you're doing* is what is running through my mind. *You would have a better shot at figuring it out than most people here*, I think, but then argue with myself. *Really? Isn't that kind of arrogant?* What I end up saying is, "Sure! I can try!"

A dozen college students climb out of a small bus that has just pulled up to the side of the road. They stand tightly together at the door, squinting in the sunlight. Motorcycles buzz past the other side of the bus as an authoritative Togolese man starts to herd the students closer to the shop that sells carvings of giraffes and African women with baskets on their heads. One of the students notices me and stops to stare.

I walk toward him, kicking up dust from the unpaved road with my falling-apart flip-flops and putting a can of Coca-Cola into my backpack. His lacrosse T-shirt hints that he is American, so I call out to him over the din of motorcycle taxis and vendors promoting their wares:

"Hey! Where are y'all from?" He stands frozen, unsure of what to make of me.

"What?"

"Hi! Where are you from?"

"Oh! We're from America! Where are you from?"

Now I am the one staring. I am wearing cargo shorts and a T-shirt, with a bandana holding my hair off my face. I had used the word "y'all." I have been in Togo for only three weeks. Do I really look that un-American?

"I'm from America, too—northern Virginia, actually."

"Oh, cool! I'm from Jersey," he says. Some other students begin to collect behind him.

"What are you all doing here?" I ask.

"We're here to help the people of Pya," another student proudly declares.

"Nice. How?" I ask, becoming less excited about meeting this group.

"Mostly by teaching English," says another.

"Cool. So how's your French?" I say. The Togolese man who was directing them earlier is beginning to look impatient.

"What do you mean?" asks the student from New Jersey.

"Do you speak French?" Most of them shake their heads no. One or two say they took French in high school.

"Oh. Well, I'm sure you'll pick it up really quickly," I say. "Do you know any Kabiyé [the local language in the region in which Pya is located]?"

They all look confused. "What's that?"

"Never mind, good luck. How long do you have?" I say as I begin to walk away.

"We're here for two weeks, and this is our fifth day. We're on our way to Pya now."

"Right. Have fun!"

I cannot help but shake my head as I walk away and pull the can of Coke out of my bag, where it has been resting next to a notebook filled with calendars and timelines that carefully plan out each day that I have to frantically complete my project. *Almost half their time gone!* I think. *They haven't even started.*

Sitting on the roots of a giant tree, trying to hide from the sunlight in as much shade as we can find, I gaze longingly at a Mitsubishi pickup truck that is parked in front of us, daydreaming about how much simpler life would be if we had our own vehicle to get where we need to go instead of relying on local taxi drivers and buses. The silence is broken when my partner asks our professor a question about running the cyber business once we have installed the materials we need. He looks at us skeptically. "You still think your materials are going to come through?" he says. Suddenly it feels as if the heat has disappeared and been replaced by intense cold. "We should have at least a week to build everything," I say, almost defensively. "If everything gets through customs, that would be a miracle," he replies. He tells us that when another student's father tried to import tea seeds for a cash-cropping project in the area, customs officials held up the shipment for months. Eventually, someone in the Ministry of Agriculture had to be bribed to get the seeds through customs. "Maybe your shipment will be different," he says, "but I would start to prepare myself."

Is my shipment "different"? My mind races as I try to think. The tea seeds would have been biologically viable. I know American customs would restrict shipments to protect local ecological systems. Togolese customs would probably do the same, right? There is no reason to restrict shipments of solar panels, though? But if officials were using that excuse only to get bribes, they could find some other excuse to hold up our shipment. Technically, our shipment is labeled potentially hazardous. We have not budgeted for bribes. We have no way to withdraw money from our donation account to pay off a customs official. Can we extend our tickets to stay longer? Will my family understand if I tell them I will not see them for another week? Another month? Can my health even last that long?

I tap my fingers on the mouse as I watch the website in front of me load at a snail's pace. When the page finally does load, it is not the "message sent" page I was expecting but, rather, "request timed out." All I want to do is send an update to my parents so they will not worry about me, but I cannot because the bandwidth in this Internet café is being used by teenagers downloading pirated movies, looking at strangers on Facebook, and watching rap videos on YouTube. *They have to pay a huge part of their income to access the Internet, and this is how they choose to use it?* Then my mind wanders to all the times I have slept through classes or chosen to go to a party instead of studying for a test. I have to pay a huge part of my income to attend college, and that is how I choose to spend time there?

Eventually I give up on sending the e-mail and decide it will be cheaper to make an international call than to buy another half-hour at the café. I head back to the taxi that is waiting to take me back to the village, where I am building another Internet café and somehow expect that teenagers there will behave differently when presented with the same exact opportunity.

The past few days have been a whirlwind. We were unable to contact the person handling our materials shipment for a few days; then we were notified that our material was waiting for shipment; then that our shipment was organized incorrectly and had to be renegotiated. Now, with only eight days until I am supposed to fly back to the United States, my partner and I are in Lomé, waiting for our shipment to clear customs.

"Prof" has instructed us to go nowhere near the airport. He is in the north for now, helping to organize a conference with two other students. His friend Henri is helping us with our shipment, using his government connections to speed things along. Customs officials could release our materials today. They could hold them for another month. We have no way to know.

Since we arrived in Lomé two nights ago, we have purchased everything we need that is not waiting for us at the airport: a generator, batteries, sealant—all of it found at the Grand Marché and waiting for us at Prof's place. Today is the Fourth of July, so my partner and I will be celebrating by going out to dinner with the two Duke students who are conducting research in Lomé. As we get ready to leave, she gets a call on her cell phone. It is Henri. I wait anxiously as she speaks to him in French and paces the room. When she is done, her back is turned to me. "What did he say?" I ask. She turns, a smile stretched across her face. "That we're leaving for Farendé in the morning. Our supplies cleared customs this afternoon."

It is Monday. By Saturday I will be sitting in an Olive Garden restaurant thousands of miles away surrounded by my family and dozens of strangers, all speaking English. I will be sleeping in an air-conditioned room in a

7.1 Under construction.

condo in a neighborhood of identical buildings all linked by paved streets, lit by electric light, and inhabited by people who will see me walk by and think nothing of it. It is mind-blowing.

By Wednesday, the piles of hand-milled wood, shoddily filed nails, and equipment scattered across the building that I now sit outside will become the most advanced technical setup this area has ever seen. If only I can put it all together.

I look down at my hands, which are covered in dirt because I had no time to shower this morning. I managed only a few hours of sleep and did not wake up for my alarm. It had been a long night of work in what Elie was now referring to as "Centre Liberté." I look down at my knees and notice how distinct they are from my legs. I have been losing weight since we arrived and am unsure of how much more I can afford to lose. Will I be able to do the work that is needed?

I have not looked over my notes in weeks—at how the circuits need to be wired. I had been focused on water lines and business plans, shipping details and customs fears. Now, one mistake could ruin a critical component we have no way to replace. I am not sure that I have brought enough

7.2 Lifting panels.

wire to complete the circuits. I am not sure the generator we bought from the store that was putting Honda stickers on knock-off merchandise will actually work, even if the store was one of the most trusted in the city. I am not sure of anything anymore.

Elie's motorcycle rolls over the field as he shouts, "Hello!" Today we are going to Kara to pay for a technician from a telecom company to come and install the Internet connection equipment for the computers. Because Elie can only take one person on his bike, my partner will stay behind and try to lead the construction effort. I will go with Elie to negotiate with the technician. Before a few days ago, my partner had hardly hammered a nail; now she will be in charge of a construction crew while I, barely able to communicate at a toddler's level in French, and Elie, whose English is sketchy, at best, will attempt to finesse an agreement with someone on whom we are completely reliant for the success of our project.

The technician stands in the middle of the room that one day will house the center's library, his bright white company polo shirt standing out in the dust that covers everything. He has come on a flashy motorcycle with an assistant, bringing almost none of the equipment we asked him to bring.

Yesterday, Elie and I tried to pay the agreed-on price for the connection service and equipment. One of Prof's assistants organized the agreement months before. However, the company now claims there is a problem: a cable is missing and will need to be shipped from Burkina Faso, the country north of Togo, which will take at least two weeks. It is a very special cable that I will not be able to find anywhere in Togo.

Later that afternoon, the technician informs Elie and me that he has an extra cable, but it is his own, personal cable. To part with it, he will need at least ten times the normal price. Again, he assures us this unique and important piece of the system can be found nowhere else. As I plug in a cable that Elie and I found at a computer supply store, the technician crosses his arm and sighs. It is a serial-USB connection. He tries to convince us that the cable I have is insufficient and that we still need to buy his cable for ten times what we paid for the one we already have. To demonstrate, he presses a button on the device connected to the computer, with no effect.

"The computer is showing that it is connected to a serial device, but it hasn't identified what the device is yet. Can you ask him if he has a software driver?" I ask my partner. She looks at me, eyes wide open and mouth shut tight. Her French has gotten us through life in Togo for weeks, but before we needed to say things like, "I would like spaghetti for dinner" and "We will be back at sunset." Now that she is the person in the village with the best combination of English and French skills, it is becoming more and more apparent what a long shot finishing will be.

She manages to make Elie understand what I am trying to say; Elie passes the information along to the technician. In response, the technician taps his chin a few times and then simply says, "Je n'ai pas le logiciel" (I do not have the software). He does not address Elie, an African man who grew up in the rural village in which we are now standing. He does not address my partner, a woman. Instead, he addresses everything he says to me, the white American man. I am the one he perceives as being the most important. I am the one he perceives as being worthy of his time.

I am furious—not only because through his bias he is unintentionally keeping us from getting what we need, but also because he is purposefully being obstructive. A flash drive hangs around his neck. It is the same flash drive that was plugged into the computer when he was demonstrating the system the day before. The driver must be on there. Elie convinces him to let us use the flash drive. It has a 4 GB storage capacity, and the technician has taken full advantage of that. Documents, songs, movies, pictures, all totally unorganized, are listed in French on the screen in front of me. "Where is the driver?" I ask. As the question is passed through the translation chain, I begin to search. *"Le logiciel est dans le cable!"* (The software is in the cable!), he shouts. He then renews his attempts to persuade us to buy his cable.

I search for the name of the manufacturer of the device on the flash drive, hoping the driver has the same name in its file address. The results pop up: one picture and one file without an identifying extension. It automatically opens as a text file and displays code. I change the extension to .exe and tell the computer to execute it. The command window pops up and begins to stream functions. *This has to be the driver,* I think. But it still does not work. *This can't be happening.* The technician is actually smiling when he sees the disappointment on my face.

My hands shake as I try to fit the wires into the right slots in the charge controllers hanging on the wall of the computer room. I am not sure whether it is caused by muscle fatigue from helping to haul the solar panels onto the roof earlier, my body still being weak after rejecting the contaminated water I drank that morning and later threw up behind the building, or because our taxi driver has already been waiting thirty minutes for us to leave for Kara, and we have hours to go.

Elie has been gone for most of the day on a series of errands. Two of the other Duke students had USB devices for connecting to the Internet via our cell-phone network, but they require steep monthly payments to remain activated. The chances of the cyber remaining profitable while making these payments is slim to none, so my partner and I have purchased several months of credit to keep the business afloat until we can come back to figure out something else to get the computers connected.

Lights hang from the newly installed rafters in the computer room, but to turn them on and off someone has to insert or pull a wire into or from an alligator clip and the battery terminal. Whenever this is done, the whole system sparks, and bits of frayed wire go flying.

Something in front of me catches my eye. A green light has begun steadily blinking on the charge controller. The batteries are charging. The solar panels work. The system is connected. I stumble over to the laptops. Each one

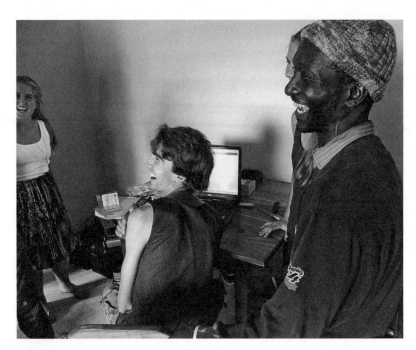

7.3 First connection at Farendé's cyber café.

is plugged into an inverter that is now humming as its fan combats the oppressive heat. Each one now shows that it is charging. We have done it. Technically, at least, everything is working.

Hours later, I am at a bar in Kara. A waitress has just come out to get our orders and starts to stare at me. She says something in French, but I cannot even try to understand her. I look at my partner, automatically expecting her to translate for me, without so much as a please. "She says you are the skinniest white man she has ever seen. She wants to bring you a beer. Do you want one?" I answer, "Does she have any soda?" My partner raises her eyebrow at me. She knows I can ask the waitress that myself. "*Il y a du Coca?*" (Is there any Coke?), she asks. "*Il n'y a pas*" (There is none).

I have not had anything to drink all day. I have not had anything to eat in more than a day. I am about to get into a *quinze places* (fifteen-seater) for what could be a sixteen-hour ride, with no way to know when or where I can get more food. I need to drink something, if only for the calories. "*Il y a du Guinness?*" (Is there any Guinness?), I ask. "*Oui,*" she answers. "*Petite ou grande?*" (Small or big?). "Tell her big so I can be bigger," I say. My partner translates the joke, and everyone in the bar laughs. It feels good to be able to make people laugh, even if it is at my expense.

The waitress brings out a large Guinness Foreign Extra, and I drink it as fast as I can. There is no way to know when our ride will get here. Just as I am finishing the beer, the van pulls up. We load everything inside, climb into our seats, and head south. Soon I feel the alcohol working its way into my system. The last thing I remember is feeling sick, but not as if I have drunk too much. I am not sure whether it was the dehydration, the hunger, the alcohol, the parasite, or the stress, but the next thing I know we are hundreds of miles south, and it is pitch black outside. My body is done. Whether I have the will to keep working is irrelevant. I need to go home. It is convenient that that is exactly where I am going.

When I got back to the United States, I found out that I was dangerously underweight and had severe vitamin deficiencies. My vision and cognitive functions were both being affected by how thin I was and by what I had been able to absorb after dealing with the parasite and by unconsciously trying to kill it with round after round of antibiotics. My mom cried and tried to hold me when she caught me coming back to my room from the shower without a shirt on. My best friends still can only stare and shake their heads when they see pictures of me from back then.

Since my return, I have not been able to stop thinking about my experiences in Togo. My feelings of weakness and powerlessness in the face of so much that I want to be able to "fix," and the memory of the isolation I faced while I was there still haunt me. They have been a driving force behind what I have done since I returned, but they have also made it very difficult to interact with people I need to work with.

7.4 A small miracle.

I have become involved in the advisory councils and leadership of several organizations involved with service and international development. I have also been working collaboratively on new projects for Farendé. When I am working with people who have not shared my experiences or had experiences with international development work themselves, I am struck by their attitudes toward the subjects we discuss.

The goal of international development is to make powerful and lasting changes in the lives of real people who are just as complicated as you and me. This is not a casual task and requires more than a casual effort. The work is not easy. Most often, it is not fun. If it were, people would have done it for themselves a long time ago. There are no easy answers. There is no one solution to global problems. Having the desire to make a difference is not the same as being able to make a difference, no matter how great the desire to do so may be.

A carefully planned yet painfully optimistic idea, weeks of volunteering, even $10,000—no matter how badly the people behind these donations of time, talent, and treasure wanted them to mean something, reality did not bend. Not only did hopes for change prove fruitless, but those hopes grew to be the very thing that prevented us from seeing the foolishness in what we were attempting. If these situations had been translated to local settings, it would have been obvious that failure was imminent: less than two weeks for children to learn a foreign language when they have no way to communicate with their instructors, a $10,000 construction project with no accountability. No teacher or investor would even consider those options, yet charities make them their business every day.

It is time that people begin acknowledging the struggles associated with international development rather than treating it as some great adventure. The failures of these projects need to be accepted and analyzed rather than swept under the rug and covered up with photos of sunsets over exotic landscapes and stories of charming locals. Unless we accept that we are not doing very much good—and in many cases, we are doing some harm—we will not be able to improve.

8. Computer Classes
Sarah Zimmermann

"Are you here to use the computers?" I ask two presumably five- or six-year old, well-dressed children in French. They nod, looking at the ground. "Would you like me to help you get started?" They nod again, and I motion to them to follow me across the room and into the Farendé Internet café (also known as the "cyber"). They stood there still looking at the ground and peering up at me, so I took them gently by the hands to seat them in front of a computer. "What are your names?" They nod. "Your names?" They nod again. My eyes widen and I said, "Oh, no. . . . You don't speak French?" They nod again.

I showed the two children how to hold a mouse, and together we learned how to left-click. By holding their hands under mine, I was able to guide the mouse, and together we played the popular matching game on the computer. With time, they became regulars at the cyber.

This story is a snapshot of my summer experience teaching computer literacy classes in a small village in northern Togo in 2015—and of how I had to learn to expect the unexpected and roll with the punches. I had to create lesson plans and teach how to use a computer in French or using no words at all. I worked on my own with consistent uncertainty in a welcoming yet unfamiliar environment and had to follow my instincts. In what follows I explain how I overcame these uncertainties (and my anxieties) and stitched together a set of classes that was adapted to local needs and the local calendar.

8.1 Teaching a wordless introduction to computers.

Standing on the Shoulders of Those Who Went Before

My work as a third-generation volunteer in the Farendé Internet café was very much a continuation of the work of those students who came before. The foundation laid by Brian Tepera and Mary Elizabeth McLaughlin was critical to the classes I taught.

Brian began teaching computer classes in 2013 after he realized how little the cyber, built just one year before he arrived, had been used. In his final report he noted, "It seemed [before I came] that no youth were using the cyber that was built primarily for them . . . simply because they knew nothing about computers." Brian documented his class lessons in detail, and his manual was foundational for instruction during the second year. He achieved a milestone in transforming a dormant cyber into a learning environment that held classes twice a week with open hours for computer exploration on Saturdays.

Mary Elizabeth leveraged Brian's momentum and continued the success of classes at the cyber. The total number of students taught during Brian's inaugural year, about twenty-five, doubled to nearly fifty the second year (Mary Elizabeth's). The number of classes held per week also doubled, and Mary Elizabeth reported a consistent class size in the teens every session.

It was the breaking-the-ice familiarity with the laptops that students acquired during the first two years of classes that made all the difference for me. At least many of them knew what a computer screen was, a keyboard, a mouse—and, in principle, what the Internet was. All of this was already a start for children who had never seen a computer before.

2015

The year 2015 at the Farendé cyber presented unique challenges. The Togolese presidential election in April 2015 canceled school for a month and shifted the students' academic schedules so they were still in class and taking national exams through the first month of our stay in Togo. I accommodated this by compressing a week's worth of classes into Friday afternoons and weekends, then readjusted again after the exams concluded. Although it was still impossible for some students to come, many embraced the modified schedule of classes. They recognized the cyber's value and seized the opportunity to learn about computers even as they balanced school, family duties on the farm, and computer classes. Another obstacle on the other end of our stay was a once-in-five-years initiation ceremony that brings everything in the villages to a stop for two weeks. I was told that no one would attend classes during this period and that I needed to get all of my work in before the ceremony began, so I accelerated classes to ensure that all content areas were covered before I left.

Community outreach—to announce the Duke projects—was taken to a new level in 2015 and helped recruit many new students to the cyber classes, thanks to a charismatic director of schools.

My alarm went off at 6:30 AM, even though I had already been awake for an hour and a half—since the sun rose that morning—anxiously thinking about the presentation that lay ahead. I threw on a T-shirt; hastily wrapped a *pagne* (cloth skirt) around my waist; and made my way to a homestead next to the school. There, two other Duke students, Ebony Hargro (who was teaching the writing class) and Morghan Phillips (microfinance); our site coordinator, Fidèle Ebia; and the program's director, Charlie Piot, were waiting. Although the school building was only a short walk from the homestead, Piot insisted we drive in his car, because that is what is expected of visitors. It would give us cachet and make a stronger impression on the students we were trying to recruit to our classes. When we arrived, the students were finishing sweeping leaves off the graveled school grounds with straw brooms and started to line up for the beginning of classes: in grade order, with the youngest students on the left, and girls in front with boys behind. The Togolese flag was raised, and one of the classes was selected to sing the pledge: "*Salut à toi pays de nos aïeux / Toi que les rendait forts*" (Hail to thee, land of our forefathers / Thou who made them strong). The voices fell silent as the anthem came to a close, and the director of schools stepped in to announce the visitors. Piot introduced himself as a teacher from *les États-Unis* (the United States) who returned each year with university students to engage in small community projects. He explained that we intended to continue the work of the previous year's students in the cyber café, as well as that of the writer's collective and the microfinance project. I remember stepping forward when my turn came to speak and slowly scanning the crowd, seeing expectant faces, faces of students who were already bored, faces of strangers older and younger than me, and a few recognizable faces of my host family members and their friends. With as loud a voice as I could manage, I introduced myself as the cyber teacher with the goal to hold classes for beginner, intermediate, and advanced computer users.

Then, suddenly, from behind me came a booming, though reassuring, community voice: "You know, if you are going to be someone in this world, you are going to need to know how to communicate. Computers are the language of the world today so you better show up at these great and free classes." This was the director of schools, a large-bellied, jovial man whom everyone seemed to respect. He insisted on the value of this opportunity for everyone but stressed that it was especially important for the eighteen-to twenty-two-year olds in their last year of high school. They would soon be asked to type their assignments at the university, so it was imperative to learn these skills now. The director's speech endorsed the cyber classes and set a fire in many to attend.

Sign-up day came two days later at the Centre Sociale, an open room with a tiled floor. Imagine the energy in this room where more than a hundred kids sat and fidgeted in chairs, waiting to enroll to learn the "language of today."

Let the Classes Begin

Students of every age anywhere in the world can tell you that there are good classes and boring classes, memorable classes and forgettable ones. To make my classes as engaging as possible, I brainstormed interactive games to introduce, demonstrate, and reinforce the key concepts I wanted my students to learn. My goal was for students to return again and again to classes and invite their friends.

Jeopardy! was my entry point. I figured the game's format was a win-win: for the students, it was an American game—a foreign novelty—and involved competition between peers; for me, it enabled informal assessment of the computer skills and knowledge the students had retained from years past. And for everyone, *Jeopardy!* was an interactive icebreaker that increased the students' confidence to take academic risks in front of their peers and a stranger, their new teacher, who had her own anxieties— among them, working toward better communication in French. There is an inherent risk in participating in such a group setting, especially for young women (who are often shy in public), but it paid off. By the end of the game, the number of students who had come at the start, fifty, had grown to

8.2 Students working during advanced computer class.

8.3 Students during open hours.

eighty, with people crowding the doorway to get a better look at what was happening at the cyber.

I built on the excitement of the introductory class and began teaching tiered classes a few days later. In years past, classes had been defined by age: youngest, middle, and older kids and adults. But I realized as we played the *Jeopardy!* game that some knowledge was not best defined by age. Some young children had attended classes the previous two years and knew answers to most of the questions, while some older ones were attending for the first time. As a result, I organized my three sections by skill level and experience: beginners, intermediates, and advanced. Each group would initially have a class on Fridays, Saturday, and Sunday, and all were invited to open hours throughout the week to work freely on material that interested them.

At the beginning, I planned my instruction class by class, focusing on learning through games and activities to demonstrate, reinforce, and informally assess the key concepts. It took several classes to understand how to show and explain in French the concepts I was teaching. Some days there was a keyboard chart on the computer at which students practiced typing their names, changing the font, changing the size of text, and using boldface and italics.

On other days, we started by playing racing games to find the letters or symbols on the keyboard. Two students would be stationed at the keyboard poster I had made; two more were at an open Word document; and everyone else used a printed keyboard to search for the letters (Figure 8.4). I called out a letter, and the whole team had to find it before moving on to the next.

It took about two weeks to create what I would consider my most useful teaching tool and secret weapon: "the List," a sequential set of fifty computer terms, including parts, definitions, buttons, and programs, that I ended up using during every class as an assessment of where the students were and to identify the next set of concepts during their class time. The List eliminated everyday lesson plans and much of my stress because it enabled me to teach to the level my students were at each day and for each class.

As I reread this sentence, I laugh, because it may appear irresponsible to be unprepared for sessions. But walking into a class with nothing but a framework was liberating and efficient, given the unpredictability of attendance during the exam period. I asked the students, no matter their age, to start at number 1 on the list: "Tell me what a computer is." Moving on to numbers 2–7, the students would identify a screen, a mouse, a keyboard, right click, left click, the cursor, and the home button. If any of these items were missed or were confusing to students, I knew where to focus my class. If these items were a breeze, I would continue on to the next part. Did the students know different computer programs and how to identify their icons? If they did know that Word is for writing documents; Paint is for drawing; Excel is for tables, graphs, and calculations; and PowerPoint is for presentations, I moved on to a more difficult set of questions about buttons on the computer, such as shift, tab, enter, delete, backspace, arrows, caps lock, and the space bar. The fourth set of questions concerned the ins and outs of Word, including font names and sizes, attributes (italics, underline, boldface), word art, shapes, and clip art. Set five included copy, cut, and paste. Set six worked through Power Point: slides, text boxes, themes, transition, and show slide show. Set seven worked through Excel: line graphs, bar graphs, and pie charts, along with calculations such as sums,

8.4 Students racing to find letters and symbols on keyboards and posters.

averages, maximums, and minimums. Only one student was able to complete the List, but for me the classes were not so much about mastering everything as they were about the students' developing familiarity with the main concepts and learning to enjoy the computer so they would be ready and willing to continue during the next class (and beyond).

I faced difficulties when too many students attended the class. Sometimes there were thirty students in a class that had only two computers. The students were frustrated that they could only work on the computer for a brief activity, and some walked out after they completed that activity, while others did not even give the class a try. I was bothered by the fact that I could not give all the students what they came for and hope that in the future we can add computers or, perhaps, a second teacher who can cover lessons that do not depend on sitting in front of a computer screen.

Despite these frustrations, the cyber slowly became a special place for me. As I became more comfortable using French computer terms and interacting with the students, with the support of the List, my nervousness dissolved and I gained a deep respect for the students' desire to learn. I spent as much time as I could in the classroom, and the students became as close to me as my host family. I thought I could stay forever, yet my time in Togo was rapidly coming to a close.

The first days of July marked some of my last in Farendé. To celebrate the hard work and learning of the students, Ebony, who taught writing classes, and I planned a final joint gala event, which we called the Exhibition of the Youth of Farendé. Our two groups would come together in a big room to read the written work of the Literary Club students and to present the knowledge of the computer students. Advertising posters were hung in the cyber, the Centre Sociale, and throughout the village to promote our event, and the news spread word of mouth through the churches and homesteads that a "party" would be held the following Friday, right before the initiations were about to start.

My students and I ended the way we began, with their favorite game: *Jeopardy!* Spirits were high with the opportunity to show off their new knowledge to local spectators and the full team of Duke students. We divided all of the students into two teams, boys and girls, and while the girls won, the score did not matter to me, because all of the students demonstrated their knowledge and had smiles on their faces. It was truly bittersweet to conclude my classes at Farendé's cyber.

8.5 Teaching beginner class.

Reflection

Looking in the rearview mirror, I consider the summer a real success. First, class participation soared to about 150 different students from Farendé and the surrounding villages Sondé and Kuwdé. This number is more than double that of the year before and five times the number of students who participated in year one. The age of the participating students widened notably with the addition of high school students (age eighteen to twenty-two) and a cohort of younger students (age five to eight). I also taught three adults privately: a village man, the middle school's math teacher, and a cyber employee. I feel that more seeds have been planted in the young generation of Farendé who have the potential to obtain genuine computer proficiency with their return to cyber classes every summer—and, I hope, in between. Finally, there were so many moments of joy for me, when the lightbulb would go on for a student who had mastered a function or a concept, in the process discovering the pleasures of the computer.

Even with this year's successes, much remains to be done. The connection is still intermittent, which limits work we can do on the Internet. There will be work to do with the new partner cyber in the mountain village of Kuwdé, thanks to the work of a fellow student, Isaac Keohane, who helped install it. A standard curriculum between the two could establish a path of learning and track students' progress from year to year. Finally, the task always remains of refurbishing computer content, finding new educational games, and putting all programs into French.

Passing on the "Language of Today"

When I am asked, "Sarah, what did you do with your summer?" the answer is a little hard to articulate. I became a teacher of more than 150 Togolese children and young adults in a rural village. I played *Jeopardy!* and many other games with my students. I learned how to communicate computer skills in French and even with no words at all. I watched a man older than me type on a computer for the first time. Perhaps the director of schools put it best: my summer was about helping a few children in a remote West African village learn the "language of today."

9. Microfinancing Teens

Emma Smith

I spent summer 2013 in Farendé, Togo, setting up a microfinance program for young adults. This meant I spent fifty-six warm and humid nights sleeping on a straw mattress under a mosquito net in a modest homestead in the middle of a valley between two small mountain ranges. Some nights there were rainstorms that were so loud it seemed as if they would crash right through the tin roof above my head. Other nights, the only sound I heard was the newborn baby giggling or crying in the small mud home across the field from my homestead. Most of these nights become a blur as I glance back at them nostalgically—except one.

I had been in Farendé for only a couple of weeks and was just beginning to get used to my frequent shuffle across the dirt courtyard in the dim middle-of-the-night starlight to the latrine. This night in particular I stumbled half-asleep out of my room and into the courtyard. As I did this, I heard the sound of papers rustling, an unusual sound for this time of night. Before I had a chance to think again, my oldest homestay sister, Viviane, pointed her flashlight toward me. I could vaguely see her outline in the dark; she was sitting on a wooden bench in the middle of the courtyard, reading. I approached her and in my broken French tried to ask what she was doing awake at this hour. She said she was studying for her upcoming school exams and did not want to wake her siblings and family, who had to get up early to work in the fields. Her studies were important; she wanted to do well on her exams because she felt that was the only way she could escape the village to pursue her aspirations. Together we spent close to an hour discussing the economic opportunities and incentives available to her. She explained that she did not want to work in the fields or to sell local beer her whole life, the way many women in the village did. She was an ambitious young woman and felt that the only way to achieve her dreams was to leave the village and her home.

As the summer went by, I began to realize that Viviane's mind-set reflected that of many young adults—that Viviane was not alone in wanting to leave and that youth flight was one of the most prevalent issues in the village. But while young adults might leave with hopes of making money or finding adventure, many would also return empty-handed.

I had been aware of this issue before arriving in Togo. A Duke student the summer before, Maria Romano, had focused on youth migration, and I had read as much as I could about migration throughout West Africa before coming to Farendé. But I did not quite realize its magnitude until after I arrived. Still, I wondered whether there might not be a solution to this issue, one confirmed by my late-night encounter with Viviane: setting up a microfinance program for teens. I imagined that the provision of small loans to young adults to create enterprises in the village might provide an incentive for them to stay in Farendé instead of migrating and give them opportunities beyond those already at hand.[1]

I also realized, however, that all of my best-laid plans—all of the research on youth migration I had done before coming, all of the reading about setting up microfinance schemes, all of the blueprints I had drawn up—would have to be thrown out the window. Before I arrived in Farendé, I had no idea about the complexities of youth migration or youth culture. I also did not know a thing about local economic principles or how local businesses were run. I had no idea that generating relationships through financial transactions were as important as realizing a profit. Surely, I now realized, I would need to understand all this before I could hope to implement a successful program in microfinance. So that is what I started to do.

Sociological Context

I look back on the first weeks I was in Farendé as an adjustment period—for my body to become familiar with the intensity of the climate and the flavors of the food, for my rusty French language skills to improve, and mainly for me to begin to understand the local culture and the context in which my project would take place. I also had to earn the trust of community members and learn to begin to build relationships in the way that they did. Needless to say, these weeks were a slow moving part of my summer—and a time that I questioned whether my project would have the capacity to make a difference at all. I even became discouraged that I would be able to set anything up at all because I knew so little.

Although things did not look bright at the time, my professor encouraged me to immerse myself in parts of the village that related to my microfinance project. So I began learning about small businesses, hanging out in the weekly market and having conversations with young adults about commercial opportunities. I soon realized that if I could begin to ask questions and make observations to understand what peoples' overarching economic goals were and how economic principles operated locally, I might be able to see how to create a microfinance program that would work.[2] Through this process I came to learn that three principles motivated the way many business transactions took place in Farendé, and all were tied up with personal relationships. I call these principles loyalty, reciprocity, and reputation.

The first of these—loyalty to friends and clients—I discovered by visiting the weekly Saturday market. This crowded, bustling, colorful cornucopia of small businesses set up side by side in a dusty yard was where I collected most of my qualitative data, which later helped conceptualize the principles that the microfinance program we set up would encompass. Initially, though, asking questions and making observations in the market only confused me more. I remember asking a woman who sold rice how she differentiated her enterprise from those of her thirteen competitors, who were sitting next to her. All she replied was, "My rice is simply better, so people will buy it." And she was right—they did. But this reasoning ran counter to my economic sense: why would vendors of the same product be sitting next to one another? It would be like going to the mall and seeing thirteen shoe stores in a row. The fundamentals of commerce here seemed

9.1 Young women selling goods at the market.

different from what I was used to. People seemed to be relying on relation-ships, returning to those they knew and trusted, rather than on quality or price (although they were discriminating in these areas, as well; all things being equal, they preferred lower prices and higher quality). I recall a simi-lar conversation in which I asked a woman selling salt and other spices how she attracted customers. She replied, "I tell my friends to buy their spices from me, not from the other sellers in the market." Sure enough, this worked: by the end of the day, her entire supply had disappeared.

Again, this seemed counterintuitive to me. In markets in the United States, sellers try to differentiate themselves, often through branding and advertising, to sell their goods. But these concepts seemed not to apply in Farendé's weekly market. In their place was a system of personal relation-ships and loyalty to friends. It seemed that as long as the buyer and seller trusted each other, and the quality of the food item was high, a lot was in place for a successful transaction to occur.

The second guiding principle was reciprocity. I noticed that this was important during my very first days in the village, when all of the Duke students who spent the summer there went to meet the village chief. As we sat under his thatched bungalow, he offered us guidance for our weeks in

Farendé: "You will learn from us, and we will learn from you. One person alone can achieve nothing." He illustrated this by saying that when people farm, they do it in groups; they help one another. When they perform ceremonies, they receive help from family and friends. When one person helps another, the other should return the help.

This sort of reciprocity was practiced inside the market and out and seemed essential to forming relationships. I saw it at play when I went with my homestay sister Viviane to the weekly market. Once we arrived, she quickly navigated through the vegetable sellers with their fresh goods arranged neatly on the ground, wove her way through the piles of calabashes for sale, and rushed by the young men selling live animals to get to the area where beer was sold.

Once there, she scanned the beer sellers, apparently looking for someone in particular, while gently waving for me, still stumbling, trying to hop over chickens and ducks under thatched stands to get to her. By the time I did, Viviane had found a friend's beer stand, a friend whom she later explained had been helping her learn to cook a certain dish in her spare time. It was important that Viviane reciprocate her friend's cooking lessons by buying beer from her in the market.

I quickly had to learn to practice this concept myself. I had gone out for a run one evening after a rainstorm and returned home with shoes caked in mud. As I stood at the well filling a bucket with water for a shower, I noticed my six-year-old homestay sister, Adeline, picking up the muddy shoes I had just shed. She was playful and always coming up with new games, so I gave her a smile and thought nothing of it. When I emerged from the cinder-block corner of our homestead that was our shower area, however, I found my running shoes sparkling clean because little Adeline had been scrubbing them. As she returned my earlier smile, I recalled the notion of reciprocity from talks with my professor. In cases such as this, you do not pay people for their help. You reciprocate with a gift that you deem appropriate. In this instance, I gave Adeline something in return for her thoughtful action.

The third key principle was reputation. While interviewing a group of young women about their travels to Benin and Nigeria, one admitted shyly that her friend had gotten involved in sex work during her time in Benin. She seemed to know that if this became known, people would look down on her friend when she returned, so she spoke in a whisper about the friend and never mentioned her name. From this moment, I began to understand that a person's reputation in the village was his or her livelihood. My home-stay mother, Justine, further exemplified this principle only days later while she was selling beer at the homestead. These drinking sessions usu-ally became social events. One lively man in particular always seemed to come around to drink Justine's beer, once commenting to me, "It's the best in the village." He had a loud sense of humor and a belly laugh that echoed to neighboring homesteads. The second he arrived, the party seemed to begin, and other beer drinkers immediately seemed to enjoy themselves more. My homestay brother Victor was the one who pointed out to me that the man never actually paid for his beer. But Justine was not about to force his hand. Week after week he left saying, "I owe you. I'll pay next time." But the next time never seemed to come. Yet Justine, knowing the sense of camaraderie this man brought with him, and knowing that shaming him publicly for nonpayment might damage her in the eyes of others, chose not to compromise her reputation for revenue. She just laughed off his lack of payment for the beer, time and again.

In short, my excursions into the Farendé marketplace and into the world of Kabre personal lives convinced me that I would have to take ac-count of local economic principles and practices that depended so much on personal relationships and issues such as reputation and reciprocity to design a successful local microfinance scheme. Trust seemed essential to Kabre culture, and I had to earn and understand it. That is what I set about doing.

Outreach

As I spent my first three weeks in the village doing the background research needed to begin my project, I also worked on the side to generate interest in the microfinance program. I did this with a dynamic young man named Cyril, who ran the Actions Sociales community center in Farendé, which would later become the meeting place for our microfinance sessions. In retrospect, the microfinance program would never have come to fruition had it not been for the confidence, commitment, relationships, and ideas that Cyril brought to the table. He was also essential in helping me to com-municate with and hold meetings and information sessions for young adults interested in pursuing microfinance.

The first meeting was held a week and a half into my time in Farendé. About a hundred students and young adults in the village filled the large, open-air room of Actions Sociales, and most seemed eager to learn about the opportunities we were about to share. After Cyril introduced the idea of microfinance, we fielded questions and asked who might be interested in signing up by project type. Nearly twenty-five people age fourteen to twenty-five put their names on a wrinkled sheet of paper. Although I was glad to see that people were excited about the program, I began to get nervous, because at this point I was not sure where this was going to lead.

After that realization, I began to write observations in my journal more frantically about the economic and subsistence practices of the village. I made maps of the weekly market and would sit next to my homestay mother as she cooked dinner each evening on a handmade wooden stool by the open fire, asking her question after question about where she bought every ingredient of the dish she was cooking. Here I also learned that she was incredibly loyal to her vendors and that reciprocity and reputation mattered at each step along the supply chain.

Much of my anxiety subsided when, a week after the first meeting at Actions Sociales, we held a follow-up session with the young adults who had expressed an interest in participating in the program. Nearly every individual who had put his or her name on the sign-up sheet was in attendance—a few with babies tied to their backs, and others with notebooks on their laps—all eager to learn more about the opportunity. Cyril began to explain in more detail the process of receiving a loan, then paying it back over time while creating or building a business, as the students, young mothers, and entrepreneurs excitedly took notes. Toward the end of the meeting, people began raising their hands and sharing ideas for small enterprises. One young man wanted to create a business raising and selling chickens, while a group of young women said they wanted to sell sorghum beer in the market. As I listened to these individuals state their ambitions, I began to see that it was the work of the young men and women of the village, not my own, that would make this microfinance program flourish.

After that session, I also began to redirect my efforts. I spent less time learning about the broad scope of economic activity in the village and more on what young adults were doing, economically and otherwise.

The young men spent their days in the fields in cohorts and the evenings, often drinking and socializing. Young women tended to stay in or

9.2 Young women preparing a meal in the homestead.

around the homestead for much of the day and spent their time cooking, cleaning, and caring for young children. Yet despite their different societal roles, young men and women had in common a desire to leave Farendé in search of other opportunities.

After the sun set in my homestead, we would dance and sing along to local songs that played on the radio. About halfway through my time there, my homestay brother Nathan showed up with a radio that took a memory card. He had loaded the card with his favorite music—a number of American and Nigerian songs. The young women and men in my homestay were ecstatic, saying they no longer had to listen to Togolese music. They all seemed to crave this bit of foreign culture, a taste of the other that also gave them a desire to travel.

I recall another night, when Nathan arrived from the fields with a book in his hands. He was moving slowly, and Justine explained to me that he had

9.3 Fifteen-year-old Victor working in the fields.

contracted malaria. Yet it was the night before he was supposed to take his exams for school, so he did not stop studying. He persisted, saying, just as Viviane had told me earlier, that he knew that these tests were his ticket out.

I reasoned that, like Nathan and the young women in my homestead, most of our prospective clients were spending their time among home, school, and the fields. They spent their days harvesting and cooking, studying for school, and socializing after sunset.

Many had made previous trips to Benin, Nigeria, or the south of Togo. We spoke with one young man who had traveled to Benin twice to work in the fields. He returned after one summer with a motorcycle and after the other with cash. Another I spoke with, a young woman who was not quite so fortunate, came back empty-handed after a summer of work in a retail store in Nigeria. Her boss had refused to pay her at the end of the summer, and she quickly learned that the principles of loyalty and reciprocity that held true in the village were not necessarily applicable elsewhere. The youth of Farendé all seemed to have stories like this that they shared, just as they shared desires to leave.

Most also had little experience living independently or sustaining themselves alone. They lived interdependent lives in the village, with men depending on women and women on men (in feeding the family). But this also made them vulnerable when they traveled. Stories circulated about people who had trusted strangers who had taken advantage of them.

It became evident that understanding all the complexities of the social and work lives of young adults in Farendé was a difficult, although important, task. I was especially glad to have gained a better understanding of how women's and men's roles and work differed. This enabled me to help potential clients brainstorm business ideas accordingly. Still, I wrestled with how I could best support the prospective clients of the microfinance program as they came up with business ideas, budgets, and plans.

By the end of the second meeting, we had given the aspiring entrepreneurs what we thought was a simple assignment: to create a budget for their enterprises. We gave little instruction, assuming that these individuals understood how to create budgets to plan for their ventures.[3] As we got the budgets back, however, we realized the mistake we had made in giving such vague instructions for the assignment. The budgets we received mostly consisted of the name of a prospective client and a few numbers that reflected the cost of the supplies he or she would need. No one considered transportation, location, pricing, expected profit, or other factors that all seemed important in starting a business. Although there were hints of what I would call financial forecasting, many applications focused more on who would help them out with their enterprises and who would help if things went wrong. This was another example of how important relationships are to this economy and trump principles that a Duke economics major might think are more important. For example, many budgets highlighted which family or community members were going to help. Another difference: the assumption that things might go wrong (because enterprises fail, just as the crops fail when the rain does not come) is risk-averse behavior (thinking about how you will cover your losses in case of failure) rather than risk-valuing behavior (that is, the sort of behavior a Duke economics major might want to encourage). This was one of the many moments during the summer in which I was reminded that no matter how much I had prepared, there were still going to be things that caught me by surprise. At these times, what seemed to matter the most was how I responded to the unexpected.

When we received the budgets and realized they were lacking from a forecasting perspective, my professor's assistant, Mackenzie, a doctoral candidate in anthropology, and I got together and brainstormed a workshop that would teach the prospective loan clients how to create a more complete budget and plan a business venture. We created a six-page document that contained questions such as, "Where will you be purchasing your supplies?" "How many times a week will you be selling your goods?" and "Who are your customers?" We also asked each person to calculate expenses, revenues, and profit margins. While we gave the prospective clients the template, we also felt it was important to acknowledge local principles and not just impose ours. So we also asked who they might call on in times of need.

Helping Clients Calculate Costs and Profits

During the workshop, we decided to run a simulation of market activities to help prospective clients familiarize themselves with calculating transactions. The simulation consisted of some individuals selling goods such as gum or candy for set prices, and other individuals serving as consumers buying these goods. Through this exercise we hoped to demonstrate the importance of thinking through the consumer's eyes, of understanding his or her needs.

When the time came to hold the workshop, Mackenzie and I were prepared with candy in our pockets and handouts, printed at a copy shop an hour outside the village, tucked under our mosquito-bitten arms. As usual, most people arrived late—they had household chores that were deemed more important—but eventually seventeen of the twenty students were in attendance and listened intently as we moved through the budgeting process.

After all of the details of budgeting were explained and questions had been answered, the prospective loan clients appeared to have a better idea of how to move forward with their businesses. They left the meeting conversing excitedly with one another about their projects, with their budget worksheets tucked under their arms. That night, as I walked home down the dusty road of the village, I waved to the circles of women cooking outside their mud homes and greeted the men cultivating in the fields with a hearty *Alafia-we?* (Your health?) and newfound sense of confidence, believing for the first time that my project might make an impact on lives in this quietly inspiring village.

Establishing MJF Principles

After we had done our educational outreach in the Farendé community, those of us working on the initiative—Mackenzie, Cyril, my professor, and I—began to formulate the operating principles of how we wanted to implement the microfinance program, which we decided to call Microfinance des Jeunes de Farendé (Microfinance for the Youth of Farendé; MJF). We first decided what we wanted the program to achieve; then we set about deciding how to set up a scheme that could be successful. We wanted something that would make a difference in the lives of youth—a program that would offer young adults the support, encouragement, and financial services they needed to start small businesses—and we wanted something that would be sustainable and accountable. We thus began jotting down notes about

9.4 A woman repaying her loan at the FUCEC meeting.

operating principles, then met to brainstorm and think them through. But we were still getting stuck on how to best implement them.

At one meeting, Cyril suggested we attend a gathering of a Farendé women's microfinance group that was run by an organization called FUCEC. The group of twenty met every Tuesday afternoon in the mud gazebo behind Cyril's office to discuss and repay their loans. As he described the successes and self-sustaining nature of the small group, I became interested in learning how they had made it work. When Tuesday afternoon came around, I arrived at what I thought would be a prompt hour—ten minutes late—to the meeting. To my surprise, the women were already well under way in discussing their transactions. The women were not only prompt; they were organized, timely, and strategic as they went about paying back heaps of cash and noting them in ledger entries. (Each woman kept a booklet showing her loan amount and outstanding balance.) This gave us the idea to create booklets for our clients, as well, as a way for them to keep track of their payments and manage their finances.

At one point during the meeting, a group of women began yelling at a younger woman in the group. Since they were speaking Kabre, I could not understand what they were saying, but Cyril later explained that they were

9.5 Booklets used by clients of FUCEC.

chastising the young woman because she had missed a payment for the second week in a row. This was another example of the principle of reputation being important. Since the group is unable to levy a fine on someone who has defaulted on a loan, peer pressure—public shaming, threat to reputation—is used to ensure that loans are repaid in full and on time. This was a strategy we later implemented in the MJF.

The women in the FUCEC program were critical to helping us come up with principles and strategies that would best fit the community of Farendé. They are the pioneers of microfinance in the village, and they will be fundamental to the long-term success of the MJF, as well. Their shared knowledge and contribution to our efforts have been invaluable.

Another microfinance program that helped us formulate principles for the MJF was COOPEC, which is based in the town of Kara, about an hour away from Farendé. My professor and I met with the director to discuss the secrets to COOPEC's success. (We had discovered that each microfinance program operates according to slightly different principles—that is, they all have their "secrets"—and drawing on their experience helped us think through our efforts.) COOPEC had a well-organized outreach into nearby villages—and was accustomed to making frequent visits to the homes of those the program financed—and an impressive repayment rate (95 percent) on its loans. The director explained that she felt the program's success was due largely to its interest scheme, in which clients paid 10 percent interest on top of their loan repayments. Half of this interest, however, actually went into a savings account that was kept for the client. After paying back the loan and interest in full, the client received the additional 10 percent he or she had paid back as interest. If the client defaults on the loan, however, he or she is unable to receive this money. We decided to include this clever incentive strategy in our microfinance initiative.

With the help of FUCEC and COOPEC, we were able to formulate a plan for the MJF. We carefully thought through the principles of repayment, knowing that they would determine our success or failure:

Repayment Principles

- Each client will be responsible for repaying his or her given loan
  - Each individual will receive a different size loan, ranging from $10 to $100
  - The client will sign a contract with a repayment schedule

- 10 percent of repayment is "interest" due, a sum which will go into a savings account for the client
  - Only after the client has repaid the loan in full can he or she receive this sum
  - If the client defaults on the loan, he or she does not receive this interest
  - If the client chooses to take out another loan after repaying the first one, the interest he or she made on the first loan is reinvested in the next loan
- Clients will be clustered into groups of up to five people
  - Each group will be based on similarities in project and repayment schedule
  - All clients in a group will repay on the same day and time
  - Most will repay every week, although some will have longer repayment trajectories so we can remain flexible and accommodate diverse projects
  - No one in the loan group can take out another loan until everyone in the group has paid back
- Clients should document their payments in their ledgers to track their own progress and debts
  - Each individual project will have its own booklet
  - Cyril will keep a copy of the repayment records in a book in the event that a booklet gets lost or ruined

Selection of Clients

After the principles of the MJF were established and the infrastructure was created, the next step was to select the clients. At this point, we had a stack of completed budget worksheets from people who hoped to participate in the initiative. Each individual had carefully completed the worksheets after the workshop and returned them to Cyril's office a few days later. After looking at the revised budgets, we decided to conduct interviews with each potential fundee. This was an important step, as it was through the interview process that we were able to find out more about the project and more about the person behind the project. Here Cyril was key because he knew most of the teenagers and their families, and he had a sense of their reliability.

While many prospective clients had submitted detailed and accurate budget proposals, some did not demonstrate during the interview a detailed understanding of all of the essentials necessary to make their projects a success, although we worried that their nervousness might have interfered with their ability to express themselves clearly and confidently. Others came with the opposite—a weak written budget proposal but a bold spoken confidence about the project.

By the time the four of us sat down to discuss our finalists, we felt we had a strong enough sense of each of our seventeen applicants and that we were able to make well-informed choices. We decided to give out seven loans to individuals we felt were strong-willed, confident, and determined. The projects ranged from making local beer and peanut sticks for sale in the market to buying fertilizer cheaply and reselling it at a profit and raising small livestock. We in fact had enough money to fund more projects but decided not to, because we were unsure of those beyond the first seven and thought it best to pilot the project with a few rather than many clients. But we informed those who were not selected and other community members

9.6 Cyril (center) with local chiefs (and Emma) at the celebration.

9.7 Essotcholo, an MJF client, poses with her mother (left) after receiving her loan.

that if the selected clients paid back their loans, there would be future opportunities to borrow from the scheme.

We decided to host a small ceremony at which we announced the first clients of the MJF. In addition to the applicants and their parents, Cyril invited a couple of his superiors, and we invited the local chiefs. After the chiefs—who came in colorful, festive attire—welcomed everyone and thanked us for supporting Farendé's youth, and after Cyril's two bosses

9.8 Viviane poses with her mother, Justine, on the day she received her loan from the MJF.

gave pep talks about the importance of entrepreneurship, we announced those who had been selected to receive the loans.

Although there was obvious disappointment on the part of those who were not selected, those who were invited to participate were thrilled, and the overall tone remained celebratory, with everyone excited that we had launched an initiative focused on youth, the first time in the area that microfinance has been available to this segment of the population. Those invited to participate were applauded as they stepped forward, and various entrepreneurs and business owners in the community shared words of wisdom and support with the young visionaries. After the formalities, we distributed beer and baked goods to all and took pictures of the new participants and their parents, whom we were counting on to help in their children's businesses. In this sense, we were remaining true to local principles of the importance of family, relationship, and reciprocity in the running of businesses.

Conclusion

The most important factor in conceptualizing and implementing the microfinance program was designing it with the local context in mind. This meant, first, finding out as much as possible about youth culture and what leads teens to want to leave home. Second, it was important to learn about local economic practice by conducting research in homesteads and the local market. Third, it was useful to understand the secrets of other microfinance NGOs in the area to find out their best practices—to learn what has worked and what has not.

From COOPEC we learned the importance of house visits and building a personal relationship with clients and those close to them and of the incentive system that the NGO has built into its repayment scheme (the "interest" that clients receive once they have paid off the entire loan). From FUCEC we learned the importance of the ledger and the weekly meeting, in which group members themselves help maintain the reputation of their colleagues and ensure reciprocity and loyalty when they are remiss in making payments.

Most important, I learned to set aside some of my economic "common sense" and pay attention to local practice. Principles of reciprocity, reputation, and customer loyalty became central to the success of these projects.

Dismissing them as unimportant, or uneconomic, would certainly have led to failure.

Coda

Two years after its launch, the MJF has seventeen fundees, of whom fifteen are paying their loans back in full and on time. The other two, Cyril has written—he sends an e-mail report once a month—have what he thought were legitimate explanations (sickness, a death in the family) and have promised to continue making their repayments soon. This represents a healthy beginning, but the MJF still has a way to go before it becomes self-sustaining—fully recouping the money it lends and supporting at least a part-time employee to oversee the program.

One of the recent updates that excites me most is that my homestay sister Viviane—the one I encountered in the courtyard in the middle of the night—is among our newest clients and has received a loan. Viviane is now on her way to raising and selling pigs right at home. The only reason she will now need to leave the village is when she expands her business into neighboring Benin and Nigeria.

Notes

1. A vast literature on microfinance is available. For a range of views, both positive and negative, see, among others, Cockburn 2006; Feigenberg et al. 2011; Karim 2014; Ledgerwood 2012; Morduch 2000; Moyo 2009; Yunus 1998; Yunus and Jolis 1998.
2. "Resources for Microfinance," Togo: Country Brief, April 29, 2013. http://www .africaneconomicoutlook.org/en/country-notes/west-africa/togo/.
3. "How to Start a Business Budget," 2015. Inc.com, http://www.inc.com /encyclopedia/businessbudget.html.

References

Cockburn, Alexander. 2006. "A Nobel Prize for Neoliberalism? The Myth of Micro-loans." *Counter Punch*, October 22–24. http://www.counterpunch.org/2006/10/20 /the-myth-of-microloans/.
Feigenberg, Benjamin, Erica Field, and Rohini Pande. 2011. "Building Social Capital through Microfinance." National Bureau of Economic Research Working Paper no. 16018, www.nber.org/papers/w16018.

Karim, Lamia. 2014. "Demystifying Microcredit: The Grameen Bank, NGOs, and Neoliberalism in Bangladesh." In *Theorizing NGOs: States, Feminisms, and Neoliberalism*, eds. Victoria Bernal and Inderpal Grewal. Durham, NC: Duke University Press.

Ledgerwood, Joanna. 2012. *The New Microfinance Handbook*. Washington, DC: World Bank Publications.

Morduch, Jonathan. 2000. "The Microfinance Schism." *World Development* 28, no. 4: 617–29.

Moyo, Dambisa. 2009. "Banking on the Unbankable." In *Dead Aid: Why Aid Is Not Working and How There Is a Better Way for Africa*, 126–32. New York: Farrar, Straus and Giroux.

Yunus, Muhammad. 1998. "Poverty Alleviation: Is Economics Any Help? Lessons from the Grameen Bank Experience." *Journal of International Affairs* 52, no. 1: 47–65.

Yunus, Muhammad, and Alan Jolis, 1998. *Banker to the Poor: Micro-Lending and the Battle against World Poverty*. Dhaka, Bangladesh: PublicAffairs.

10. The Farendé Writers' Society
Caitlin Moyles

I spent two months in Farendé, a small, rural village in northern Togo, initiating and teaching a writers' society for teenagers and young adults. I taught biweekly classes at Centre Liberté, the local Internet café, where young, aspiring writers from Farendé and Kuwdé, a village just up the mountain, explored different genres of literature and practiced creative writing. With our graduate assistant Mackenzie Cramblit and local contact Jesper Karma, we helped the society members develop their creative writing skills and find inspiration in their daily lives in the villages. They also participated in discussions about a wide variety of well-known English and French literature—the poetry of Guillaume Apollinaire, Gwendolyn Brooks, and Albert Lozeau; the stories of Ernest Hemingway and John Steinbeck; and excerpts from Marcel Proust's À la recherche du temps perdu and Céline's last novel, Rigodon. They spoke with a guest speaker, Patrick Katchawatou, a published author from Farendé, and listened to a poetry reading by Elie Karma and Jesper's performance of Kabre poetry. At the end of six weeks, the students typed up final drafts of their best pieces and published them on a class website that I created with Nathalie Berger, another Duke-Engage student.[1] Finally, Mackenzie and I organized a literary salon and closing ceremony at Centre Liberté. The salon drew quite a crowd of writers' family and friends, and the writers read their favorite pieces aloud and saw the newly finished website. In English, I call the group the Farendé Writers'

Society. In French, the group is called Le Collectif Littéraire des Jeunes de Farendé, a name we brainstormed together and chose from seven options in a dramatic blind vote.

Everything I have written is true, but I smile to myself when I read that description of my summer. It sounds like I arrived in Farendé with a carefully researched agenda and that everything went according to plan. However, when I look back on my work, I am pleasantly surprised that the Farendé Writers' Society came together at all. I did not step up to the plate with extensive experience; instead, I was propelled by an idealistic fuel, consisting of a love of literature and creative writing, an advanced but imperfect grasp of the French language, and a desire to challenge myself. Here is one thing I learned from my teaching experience in Togo: when planning an interventionist project in a foreign country, no matter how firm your convictions, good your intentions, or detailed your plan, you are going to end up flying by the seat of your pants. I spent hours studying the history, geography, politics, language, and culture of my host community in an independent study with our professor the spring semester before the trip. I read about pedagogy; I got advice from the dean of undergraduate studies in education; I discussed Literacy through Photography methodology with that program's director. I could plan, but I could not foresee every obstacle lurking around the bend. In fact, I could not get answers to some very important questions until I arrived in Farendé: how many students would participate in my project? Would they be in elementary school, high school, or university? Could I engage them in French literature and creative writing? More important, how would I know if my project was "successful"? Would it be useful to the community? Would it give the students transferrable skills?

One of the essential lessons I learned was to not over-prepare. The most important learning happens on the ground, once you have arrived. Openness to feedback and adaptability, more than determination, make all the difference between a successful project and a failure. I love writing about my project with a tone of authority; however, looking back, my time in Togo was easier, more enjoyable, and ultimately more productive because I arrived with a healthy dose of uncertainty about my role there. "We'll have to see whether young people in Farendé are even interested in creative writing," our professor reminded me more than once during our independent study. I needed to be mentally prepared to drop my project and run with something else if it did not get off the ground.

In addition to adaptability, I needed a network of supporters. My seed of an idea needed nourishment from an entire ecosystem to grow. I found this support in our professor, whose background knowledge about Kuwdé and Farendé goes back twenty-five years and who knows almost everyone in the villages; in Jesper Karma, our local contact and talented linguist, who helped me with logistics for all of the writers' society meetings; in his brother, Elie Karma, an entrepreneur and poet who spearheaded Centre Liberté and lent me books from his collection for class, as well as classroom space and computer time; in Mackenzie Cramblit, a doctoral student in cultural anthropology at Duke who spent a year in Cameroon on a Fulbright scholarship and helped me lead every class and jumpstart discussion when my French failed me. I also depended on the chiefs of Farendé and Kuwdé and the Canton Chief to encourage the young people in their homesteads to come to my classes, and on Alice, who worked at the front desk in the "cyber" and always paused her work to answer my questions. Last but not least, I could not have done this without the young people who took a chance and came to the literature and creative writing classes that I, a foreigner, was teaching at Centre Liberté. The relationships you form with people once you arrive are essential to the growth of your baby seed of an idea into a reality. It really does take a village.

The Seed: Creative Writing, Reading, and Adventure

"'We like the adventure!' is the reason most youth in the villages give for migrating to work in Benin or Nigeria," our professor explained in one of our independent study meetings. It was a Friday afternoon in January, and five other students and I were seated around a table in his office in the cultural anthropology building. The six of us were preparing to spend two months in Farendé and Kuwdé, where we would start "civic engagement" projects funded by DukeEngage. Unlike most charitable foundations and nongovernmental organizations (NGOs), we had no agenda other than to learn as much as we could about the society in which we would be living; then, once we got there, to collaborate with our professor's numerous local contacts and apply the knowledge and skills we had acquired from our majors to some useful purpose for the community.

"These projects may all fail, and I'm totally fine with that," I recall him saying. "We can learn just as much from failure as we can from success."

His words seemed particularly applicable to my project. I was a junior English major, and I hoped to start a writers' society in Farendé.

I conceived my project in response to the growing trend of youth migrating from Kuwdé and Farendé to southern Togo, Benin, and Nigeria. Generally, they leave the villages to earn money during school vacations to pay for school fees, to provide family support, to pay for apprenticeships, to earn bride wealth, or to spend on "luxury" items such as motorcycles and clothing. "Adventure" and "seeing the world" are also common reasons. As I learned from my independent study and in-person interviews with young men and women in the villages, it is impossible to categorize youth migration as "good" or "bad." The risks they take are considerable and numerous, but the young migrants do gain a broader worldview, and some of them put the money they earn to important and productive uses, several of which I mentioned earlier.

Without taking a pro- or anti-youth migration stance, I imagined myself spending my childhood vacations laboring in Benin and thought about the numerous opportunities I would miss out on. Throughout my adolescence, I was lucky to spend summers playing volleyball, taking art classes, attending an academic program for high school students at Cambridge University, traveling with my family, reading new books, and eventually preparing for the SAT and writing college essays. These activities enriched my life intellectually, physically, socially, and culturally; gave me discipline, new interests, and aspirations; and helped me get into a good university. I wanted to offer youth in Farendé and Kuwdé a summer opportunity that might enrich their lives in even just a few of these ways. As an English major, I thought the best way I could do this would be to start a writers' society. I wanted young people to experience that reading and writing can be fun, to see the world without leaving Farendé, and to be inspired to dream big. I hoped that a writing club would plant the seed for a lifelong love of reading and writing in the students and young adults who did stay in the villages during the summer I would be there.

When I heard our professor say that one reason young cultivators from Farendé and Kuwdé give for leaving is "We like adventure," I was filled with growing conviction. If young people crave to see the world, they might enjoy literature and creative writing. To "get lost in a book" is to let one's mind wander, to travel to new places while sitting beneath a tree, to imagine new horizons for the first time. There was a place for a writers' society in Farendé. Young people would participate. Wouldn't they?

I had made a connection, albeit a tenuous one, between the phenomenon of youth migration and creative writing. However, throughout the semester leading up to the trip, I doubted the purpose of my project. Did I have an unconscious personal agenda? Did I want to prove to *myself* that reading and writing really do matter in people's lives, as more than just leisurely recreation? I was not able to stop doubting the value of my own project until after I had been on the ground in Farendé for almost a month.

Unsurprisingly, I still found it difficult to explain my summer plans to my extended family.

> "So, Caitlin, have your summer plans taken shape yet?"
>
> "I'm spending two months in Togo to work on a civic engagement project."
>
> "Togo . . . where is that?" was the typical response.
>
> "It's a really narrow country between Ghana and Benin."
>
> "Ah. And what will you be doing there?"
>
> "Well, a lot of youth are migrating to Benin and Nigeria to earn money during the summer, and one of the reasons they leave is that they want to have adventures and see the world. So I'm going to teach literature and creative writing to high school students. If there are more enriching opportunities in the village, young people might be more likely to stay."

Very few people had anything to say after this except, "Ah, how interesting." I can see why—stated so simply, my last two sentences sound like a non sequitur. But I thought along the same lines as our professor: it would be better to try and fail than not to try at all. If no one joined the writers' society, so be it. I would spend two months helping the other DukeEngage students with their projects.

Sociological Context

Once the Farendé Writers' Society was under way, our professor suggested that I interview students, teachers, parents, and the elderly with Jesper to get a better understanding of the culture around youth literacy in Farendé and the sociological context of the Farendé Writers' Society. Is reading perceived as uncool? Why do young people not read during their summer vacations? Why does it seem that no one reads to relax at the end of a long day in the fields? Why is it so rare for adolescents to keep journals about their daily lives? After conducting these interviews, I was finally able to better articulate why a writers' society could actually *matter* to young people in Farendé and Kuwdé.

When the community was out cleaning up the local marketplace, I asked a couple of people variations of the question, *"Pourquoi les jeunes de Farendé n'aiment pas lire pour le plaisir?"* (Why don't young people in Farendé like to read for pleasure?) One man told me that young people would read, but they lacked the means to do so—that is, books and flashlight batteries (for nighttime reading). He added that competition, such as a writing competition, would motivate adolescents to write.

An elderly woman who was involved with one of the churches in Farendé was very encouraging. She said that the relatively new high school in Farendé had changed the village's culture, and now people were more open to reading.

The chief of Farendé had a less optimistic perspective. "Young people don't read at all," he said. "Reading and writing used to be more common before cell phones because you had to write letters to stay in touch with one another. Now people use cell phones instead. And often older children in the village make fun of those who carry books around with them, which makes them feel bad, as if they are not part of the crowd."

One young man who appeared to be about eighteen and was still in middle school told me that the school often lends students the books required for class, and that he has to share them with three, four, or five other students. In this case, each student might keep the book for three days, then run it to the others' houses. He added that students sharing a book sometimes organize discussion groups at someone's homestead to prepare for exams. Surely, I concluded, this lack of books hinders productivity. But did changing the culture of youth literacy in Farendé really just come down to bringing resources to the village?

Alice, who studied history at the University of Kara and worked the desk at Centre Liberté, gave me the most insight of all. Although she never passed the exam to complete her degree, she had approached the finish line of higher education in Togo and strongly believed that reading and writing fluently in French were invaluable skills. Alice wanted to earn her degree so she could take the *concours*, an exam that university graduates have to pass to get government jobs or to work for an NGO. These are well-paying jobs in a country where it is difficult to get any salaried job at all. Reading and writing fluently in French, Alice told me, are necessary skills to pass the concours and get a job.

Alice had a lot to say about the subject of youth literacy, as well. Why do the youth of Farendé not read? "*La paresse*" (laziness), she said. Could you yourself keep a journal or write a memoir? "*Vouloir, pouvoir*" (If there's a will, there's a way). I asked whether the challenge of earning money during the summer to pay school fees makes it too difficult for some adolescents to cultivate other interests. Alice asserted that it is possible to go to school, cultivate your fields, read a little every day, work in Benin or Nigeria during the summer to earn money to pay for school, and go to the university as long as you organize your schedule and use your time well. This sounded reasonable to me, but maybe that was because it aligned with my own personal experience, culture, and background. Finally I asked her whether a lack of means—money to buy batteries for a flashlight or kerosene for a lantern to read and write at night—prevented youth from developing the habit of reading and writing in their spare time. Alice and Jesper exchanged a knowing glance and chuckled, as if this were an excuse that they hear often and did not think was legitimate. Alice reiterated that if there is a will, there is a way. Jesper told a story about his French professor giving his three-person class an assignment to memorize a ten-line French poem by the next day. Because there were only three people in the class, there was no way to skimp on the assignment without being caught. That night, Jesper held the paper near the fire, under the pot while his mother cooked dinner, to read. "Vouloir, pouvoir."

In short, community members' responses fell across the board. When asked to identify problems inhibiting youth literacy, each person pointed to something different—a lack of books and flashlight batteries, the prevalence of cell phones, a simple lack of motivation. One man thought that writing competitions might make writing popular, but this sounded, to me, like a quick fix that would not work alone. Alice implied that she thought "laziness" and lack of will to read and write were somehow ingrained in people's mind-set.

Although their answers varied, they seemed to fall into two general categories: lack of means (books, batteries) and lack of motivation (lack of competition or role models, laziness). Whether one or the other was the root of the problem, I could not tell. But it seemed as if the community needed both means and motivation for youth literacy to flourish. So I adopted a two-pronged approach. I tried to address the lack of means by setting up Elie's library in Centre Liberté in my spare time. As the first lending library in the region, it would be a significant milestone. In theory, the community would finally have free access to a relatively small collection—but a collection nonetheless—of used books.

Motivating young people to use the new resource, and to read and write on their own, would be trickier. My research suggested that they needed goals, role models, and support to become and remain motivated. I tried to structure the writers' society to address these needs. First, my professor and I thought Patrick Katchawatou, a published writer from Farendé, would be an excellent role model for young writers, so we arranged for him to speak to the group. Second, I explained my goal for the students on day one. By the end of my time in Farendé, I would set up a website where we could post their pieces, and they would be published writers. Finally, I tried to make the Farendé Writers' Society self-sustaining. I made sure to invite Jesper and Elie to our classes—perhaps they would lead the society one day—and encouraged the writers to check out books from the library and keep writing in their journals after I left. I thought of each writer as a seed. If I could capture their interest to the degree that each would continue to grow and thrive on his or her own, the young people would begin to change the scenery—the culture around youth literacy—in Farendé and Kuwdé.

My interview with Alice also opened my eyes to a broader picture. I saw that reading and writing fluently in French, which is most Togolese peoples' second language, is a key to moving up the ladder in Togolese society. Motivating my students to read and write in French could lead to practical, possibly even lucrative applications. I would be doing something that *did* in fact matter to them.

Starting a Writers' Society in a Rural Village

In the earliest stages of my project, we decided to build in incentives to keep youth interested in the Farendé Writers' Society. First, as mentioned, we got in touch with Patrick Katchawatou, a writer from Farendé whose first novel, *Le fantôme de Dèkoukou*, had recently been published by a French publishing company. We met with Patrick in Lomé at the beginning of the trip, where he gave me a copy of his book and assured me that my project could work and was worth pursuing. He suggested that the writing club target youth age thirteen to fifteen and agreed to speak at our first class meeting. At the kickoff meeting for all of the DukeEngage projects at Actions Sociales in Farendé, where Cyril pitched all of our projects to a large group of students, he cited Patrick as a local success story and promised that Patrick would make an in-class appearance. Connecting the project to a local success story, and a man who was a bit of a local celebrity, was important to piquing students' interest.

A second incentive was to use some of our DukeEngage project funds to buy club members new notebooks and pens so they could participate without incurring personal expenses. Finally, we decided to create a class website to publish all of the writers' pieces at the end. Most young people in Togo are eager to connect with people in other countries, so we wanted their work to be published online, where it could be read by a global audience. I tried to give the website a high production value, make it look professional and well made, something concrete in which the group could take pride. I wrote an "About" page that explained the project and took portraits of the authors to accompany their bios. My fellow DukeEngager Nathalie Berger took some photographs for the homepage and helped me design the website.

At the kickoff meeting at Actions Sociales, eleven students signed up for the writers' society. However, even though Patrick was speaking at the first meeting, only five students showed up. Patrick was our biggest draw, so I was dismayed to think that this small turnout could be an early indicator of low retention rates. It also highlighted the challenge of communication. How would I get in touch with the students if our meeting time or location changed? I was new to the community and did not know my way around very well, let alone where each student lived. There were no phones, no postal service, no email. Every message had to be relayed by word of mouth. Jesper helped me by visiting homesteads and telling students the meeting time and location in person. Still, I have wondered whether the six students who signed up but did not show on the first day did not get the word. In fact, when my time in Togo was almost at its end, I learned that

Cyril had told only a few teachers about the kickoff meeting. Other teachers later heard by word of mouth, and by that time my project was coming to a close.

The communication problem diminished once I had established a regular schedule for the writers' society meetings. Retention, however, was an entirely different challenge. Six students came to the second meeting (up one from the first meeting), but only three came to the third. I was feeling discouraged. With fewer and fewer students coming to class, soon there would not be any left. Two or three weeks later, however, the Farendé Writers' Society's membership had climbed to seven regular attendees. I think the turnaround was the result of a few good decisions. First, Mackenzie, Jesper, and I decided to move our sessions out of a dilapidated classroom and into the cyber's new, clean common area, where Elie had just installed a new chalkboard. I gained a couple students who showed up early to Brian's typing classes and were intrigued with the handouts and the new notebooks I had distributed. Fostering team spirit was another important element of the project. The day we chose a group name was by far the most fun class of all because everyone was so enthusiastic about brainstorming names and voting for "the one." Mackenzie introduced the beatnik snap as a form of applause after we read our work aloud in class. I think our camaraderie contributed to more regular attendance. We also appointed a team captain at the start of the project to collect everyone's pieces the day before class and bring them to my homestead. Electing a team captain gave the students ownership and investment in the group. Finally, Mackenzie and I planned a literary salon as a celebrative closing ceremony. The writers arrived at the cyber to music and dancing, read their favorite pieces aloud for friends and family, enjoyed refreshments, and saw the newly finished website for the first time. The literary salon and the website gave the writers' society a concrete and public presence in Farendé and, virtually, around the world.

My students were not the only people I had to work with, however. I sometimes negotiated with Elie for books, classroom space, and computer time. He was heavily involved in the day-to-day running of my project. He came on his motorcycle to unlock the Internet café before the scheduled afternoon opening time every time I needed to prepare for class. When I wanted to borrow a French book, schedule computer sessions for the writers to type their final pieces, or host our literary salon (closing cer-

10.1 A meeting of the Farendé Writers' Society.

emony) in the cyber, I asked for Elie's permission. Overall, we got along well. However, working with Elie sometimes led me into territory fraught with power dynamics that I found difficult to navigate. For example, I saw the three hundred or so books that were locked in his office as an incredible resource for my students. If I hoped to encourage their interest in reading and writing, what could be better than lending them books that matched their interests and writing style? Unfortunately, some people in the village had stolen a few books in the past, and Elie had closed his mini-library. He was happy to let me check out books as I wished, and even suggested that I assign the writers book reports. When I acted on his suggestion, however, I noticed that Elie supervised the checking-out process so closely that he intimidated the students who were borrowing books for the first time. He gave the impression that he was suspicious they would not return the books (which is perhaps understandable, considering his prior experience). Consequently, when Soulé, a would-be bookworm if he only had access to books, asked me to find him fairy tales to read, I found myself in the position of intermediary between the students and Elie. Elie's suspicious and controlling nature made me feel that I needed to advocate for Soulé. After Soulé returned the first two books, he asked me whether he could pick out another. I went to Elie, who was hoeing the fields outside the cyber, and explained to him that Soulé was trustworthy and that I thought he could lend Soulé another book. "When he wants to borrow a book, he needs to come to me directly!" Elie snapped in a fit of bad temper. "When you come and ask for them, it makes me look like the bad guy!" Perhaps I could have phrased my words differently, but I think the underlying issue was that the students were coming to me, a foreigner, for help instead of him. Thus, he felt I was challenging his authority over Centre Liberté.

Elie asserted his authority in other ways that I found counterproductive. Once I told the writers to come to Centre Liberté's free hours for youth on Saturday morning to finish typing their final pieces. I was troubleshooting as students typed away on Microsoft Word, some of them for the first time, when Elie came in and asked why we were using the free hours for their classwork. "The free hours are for youth to use the Internet. They can do typing later today," he said. He also pushed back about the literary salon that Mackenzie and I hoped to host at the Internet café on a Saturday evening. We had gotten Elie's approval before we told the students the time and location; nevertheless, a few days before the festivities, Elie approached us and reprimanded us for not consulting him before proceeding with our plans. "The cyber has a lot of traffic on Saturdays, and since it's so busy, I don't know if this is going to work," he said. To be frank, this was complete nonsense. We had discussed our plans with him, and because the Internet café closed at 6 PM, no one else would be there during the event. Mackenzie talked this over with Elie and got him back on board. He only demanded coaxing. Once we had discussed it with him a second time, Elie was enthusiastic. The evening of the event, he set up a generator outside the cyber, hooked speakers up to a computer, blasted upbeat music as guests arrived, and performed an impressive spoken word poem during the intermission. I did have Elie's support; indeed, I could not have done my project without him. But I had to deal with power dynamics to ensure that both of us got what we wanted.

My experience with Elie taught me to be sensitive to personality variation. Elie was a bit insecure and controlling, and he needed me to assure him that I understood he was in charge. He bristled in situations in which I could somehow be seen as more powerful than him. Working with Elie also made me sensitive to cultural premises underlying our work relationship. I was white, the race of Togo's French colonizers, in a country that gained its independence from France only in 1960. I was also a young woman, and few young Togolese women would interact with an older man with my degree of independence and confidence. Both of these characteristics could have provoked him to remind me that he was ultimately in charge. Ultimately, my few negative experiences with Elie made me appreciate how kindly he accommodated my culture most of the time. In many instances, he understood, and even expected, that I would act differently from young Togolese women. My negative experiences with him prodded me to make more of an effort to accommodate his culture, too.

I also ventured into political territory when I selected the literature and poetry to be discussed during our writers' society meetings. I felt unable to teach pieces of African literature, although there are many admirable works. I chose what I could teach: the French works and French translations of Western works with which I am familiar. I was not trying to indoctrinate my students with Western literature or anything of the sort. I simply did not feel comfortable teaching African literature to those who could call it their own. I was even more keenly aware of the West-heavy syllabus—which, as I mentioned earlier, included Apollinaire, Brooks, and Lozeau; Hemingway and Steinbeck; and Proust and Céline—when Jesper commented on it after one of our sessions. I was instinctively defensive of the materials I had chosen and was delighted when Jesper offered to perform Kabre poetry at one of our last meetings. I only hope that it did not seem like just a token gesture to a genre of literature that deserved more attention. In an ideal situation, Jesper would have been more heavily involved in selecting and teaching the material from the beginning. (He has worked for a Togolese publishing company and always made our class discussions spicier and more interesting.) However, Jesper was not able to extend his commitment beyond attending and participating in the Farendé Writers' Society meetings. Farendé would benefit from the addition of the works of African literature to Elie's book collection and the leadership of Farendé's schoolteachers in encouraging students to check them out to read for pleasure. For a library in rural Togo to lack works of African literature is a great misfortune.

Challenges

I have discussed several macro-level challenges I encountered as the Farendé Writers' Society developed. However, I would not be giving an accurate representation of my day-to-day work if I neglected to discuss the different culture around timeliness and completing assignments that I experienced every day in Farendé. Most teenagers in Farendé are cultivators first and students second. Working the fields is a necessity of life in Farendé. This was a rule of the game, and I understood and accepted it. However, the mentality that academic pursuits were of secondary importance bled into the everyday function of the writers' society. We usually met at 3 PM on Thursdays and Sundays. Typically, the first person would arrive at 3:20, and we would finally start at 3:30, even though not everyone was there. Students would sometimes continue to trickle in until 4 PM. Often, Mackenzie and I had to start without Jesper. Sometimes I had to start alone, with just a couple of students, because Mackenzie was at a meeting for another DukeEngage project or had to take a phone call. At first the students' tardiness, and the very real possibility that only two or three people would show up at all, made me anxious and uneasy about my project. How could I do anything if no one showed up? Would all of my preparation for that day's lesson go to waste? It also wounded my pride a little. I had already learned that the stereotype of "Africa time"—habitually showing up at least half an hour late to any engagement—was true in Togo, but my Western sensibilities interpreted my students' consistent and casual lateness as a sign of disrespect. It also made me feel like I was the only person who really cared about the writers' society. Eventually, I learned to swallow my pride and carry on. As frustrating as it was, I knew that Togolese consider lateness to be a part of everyday life rather than a sign of disrespect. (People are late for everything. When I attended an initiation ceremony, the initiate's uncle was more than an hour late, even though the ceremony could not start without him. Lateness is not only tolerated; it is anticipated and considered normal.) I also kept in mind that literature discussions and writing workshops with even just one student could still make a difference in his or her life; that alone would be a successful project.

In addition, some students showed habitual disregard for assignment deadlines. Of course, I understood that obligations such as cultivating and school exams would take priority over assignments for the writers' society.

One of the society members was a husband and a father. Another was a university student who lived in a different town and could come only on Sundays. This I understood. But it was challenging when most of the students showed up without having completed their assignments, derailing my plans for the workshop portion of the class. I learned to be patient and flexible and to think on my feet. Mackenzie's and Jesper's ideas and other contributions to our discussions (not to mention their near-perfect French) were also a great help when lessons did not go as planned.

To round out the list of challenges that I am certain all teachers face, I would add that one student turned in a poem plagiarized from Charles Baudelaire for one of his assignments. He was clearly not one of the strongest writers of the group, and I felt badly that he seemed to feel that he needed to do this to impress me and his classmates. After consulting with Mackenzie, I spoke with him alone one day as we waited for the other society members to arrive. I told him that his own writing was good and that he should not feel as if he needed to deceive us to do well. He did not try it again.

There were also several technical obstacles to my project: teaching in French, depending on the very unreliable Internet connection at the cyber, and my students' lack of typing skills. Although I have been taking French classes since fourth grade and spent a semester studying abroad in Paris, I had never faced the challenge of thinking on my feet and speaking spontaneously in French to the degree required by my teaching role. I had enough confidence that I could get by, however, to proceed with my plans. There was no other way to make the project work. I would face that challenge when the time came. Fortunately, most of the writers, like me, spoke at an advanced but not fluent level of French. Indeed, I think I spoke more freely in Farendé than in Paris because I was not as embarrassed to make mistakes. There were moments when I had to simplify what I wanted to say because I could not find the words or when I could not understand what a student was saying because she or he spoke French with an unfamiliar accent. Overall, though, we showed a mutual willingness to try to understand each other, and we got along very well. Also, Mackenzie and Jesper were usually there to pick up the slack or jump in when I needed help.

The unreliable Internet connection at the cyber was a very frustrating obstacle to my project. Texts to discuss in class that would take me twenty minutes to find and produce using my laptop in the United States often required two hours of starting and stopping my work as the Internet connection was lost and restarted. With no printer in the village, I resorted to writing out long texts on the chalkboard or trying to plan lessons well enough in advance to print handouts in Kara, the regional capital. I felt that it was important to give the students handouts because reading materials are so sparse in Farendé; however, I found it difficult to plan lessons a couple of weeks in advance, and we often had to do without handouts. My workflow would have been much smoother with the office supplies that I take for granted in the United States. The unpredictable Internet connection made it especially difficult for me to set up the class website. Our professor had a modem for his laptop, but it worked only in Kuwdé. One day I made the hour-long hike up the mountain to Kuwdé to work on the website with Nathalie, only to find that the laptop had twenty minutes' worth of charge left. We plugged it into the solar-powered charging station at the homestead, but there was not enough sunlight that day to charge it. We went back down the mountain to Farendé's cyber, where we found that the Internet was having a bad day. I stated earlier that flexibility is more important than determination in an interventionist project like mine, but this was one exception. The website would not have been finished in time for the literary salon if I had not spent hours at the cyber, taking advantage of twenty-second windows of Internet connection to e-mail the writers' final texts to Nathalie, who uploaded them to the website from our professor's modem in Kuwdé.

I wanted the students to type their own final drafts so they could have the "complete experience" of writing and publishing something online. However, even though some of them had been attending Brian's typing classes throughout June and July, none could type fast enough. Those who had not attended his classes barely knew how to use a computer at all. This phase of the writers' society was a great learning opportunity for the students, but learning cannot be rushed, and none of the participants were able to finish their work in the three typing sessions I had set up. (It did not help that everyone forgot about the second session.) I was left with a lot of typing to do the morning of the literary salon, which resulted in that stressful scene in which I frantically e-mailed finished texts to Nathalie, who was sitting with her laptop in Kuwdé. We finished the website, but with several prominent misspellings.

Outcomes and Conclusion

In hindsight, I think I went to Togo with a naïve vision in mind. I thought that students might choose to stay in Farendé during the summer instead of working in another country *because* Farendé had a new writers' society. Now I have seen firsthand that their need for money is very real, and that even though a passion for reading and writing would help them in innumerable ways in the future, it could not satisfy all their immediate needs. Indeed, I am certain that my project did not singlehandedly change anyone's summer plans; all of my students were probably going to stay in Farendé anyway or decided to stick around because Emma's microfinance initiative, Brian's computer classes, and my writers' society together formed an enticing package. That is great, too—it is just different from what I expected.

After a couple weeks in Farendé, I noticed that vans, loaded with young men and a few women, were still picking people up and bringing people back from southern Togo, Benin, and Nigeria each week. I realized I was

10.2 Farendé Writers' Society.

not stemming the flow of youth to Benin and Nigeria. This realization marked the beginning of my project's transformation. I became more realistic and adjusted my goal. If I could get just a few young writers to attend my classes regularly, and if they were proud of their final projects, then I would consider my project a success. As long as they were proud of their work, they would be more likely to pursue reading and writing for pleasure than they had been when I arrived.

I was grateful, too, that DukeEngage, unlike most foundations and NGOs, allows college students to be free from an agenda. I did not feel pressure to bring back positive reports about how well my initiative was progressing to get more funding. Failure was an acceptable outcome, as long as I learned something from it.

Based on the writing the members of the Farendé Writers' Society produced, I would judge my project a success. Seven regular attendees read and discussed a diverse selection of French literature and poetry, French translations of American works, Elie's performance of poetry in French, and Jesper's reciting of Kabre poetry. They each drafted, revised, typed, and published online their own creative writing. Their work appears beneath their portraits and a self-written biography on the Farendé Writers' Society's very own website. The young writers performed their favorite pieces in front of a great number of community members gathered at Centre Liberté. They were proud of what they had accomplished. I cherish the memories of Soulé asking me to find him fairy tales online, and Théo telling me when we said goodbye, "You have inspired me with your energy." Helping these young people discover their own potential was more rewarding than any work I have done.

Notes

1. The class website is available online at http://caitlinmoyles59.wix.com /farendewriterssociety.

Epilogue
Charles Piot

Two years of student projects have come and gone since the bulk of these essays were first drafted, and while the center has held steady—the health insurance scheme, the cyber, microfinance, and the writers' workshop remain staples—other projects are being added: latrine sanitation, a universal nut sheller, a second Internet café, an archival and oral history project, Zumba classes. It is the improvisatory, roll-with-the-punches nature of this work that not only makes it fresh and interesting—opening up new challenges and possibilities each year—but also lends it flexibility that larger development initiatives lack. States and nongovernmental organizations (NGOs)—bureaucratic apparatuses saddled with protocols, blueprints, and annual reports and at the beck and call of executives and funding streams back home—lumber along, with little ability to adapt to local realities. Rare is the NGO that can abandon a project in mid-stream that might not be working and begin something entirely new, switching, say, from child sponsorship to microfinance or from malaria prevention to agriculture.

Do-it-yourself (DIY) development in a neoliberal moment not only retains a nimbleness that enables it to travel (and sidestep bureaucratic inertia); it is also less costly. Student ingenuity discovered a way to make the health insurance scheme self-sustaining and to run teen microfinance on less than $500 a year. With student technicians—notably, engineering majors—eager to install the equipment themselves, setting up an Internet café was achieved at cost (with state-of-the-art solar panels and laptops purchased for less than $4,000). The latrine sanitation system, another pet engineering project that recycles human waste into biogas for fertilizer and algae for a fish pond, and whose low-intensity green profile has attracted interest from the Gates Foundation, was funded by small grants from Duke University administrators. For less than $1,000, these young engineers purchased plastic piping, sealant, and ten tons of gravel and cement. With labor donated by Farendé residents, they constructed cement algae basins and carved a fish pond from the earth.[1]

Several of the projects, and some of the more successful ones, require no money at all. The insurance scheme is exemplary. But so is the writers' project. In its second year (2014), the writers' workshop enrolled eighteen students who embraced an idea floated by the Duke student facilitator—to write a one-hundred-page novel in a month. By writing four pages a day, and never looking back, ten of the eighteen achieved their goal. Several of the novellas, especially those with a focus on everyday life in the villages, were surprisingly good. We are now bundling together the best ones to publish at a press in Lomé, where printing two hundred and fifty copies costs $500. Needless to say, these young authors are thrilled that their work will be published. And a synergy has developed: in focusing on everyday life in the villages, many wrote poignant narratives about youth leaving for Nigeria—accounts of conversations between parents and children about the pros and cons of leaving, descriptions of travails on the farms of Nigeria and in the bars of Benin. Since this migratory phenomenon is the larger context that subtends all of our projects, having local teens write about it deepens and adds nuance to our ethnographic archive.

Moreover, this turning into text of local experience has spawned another idea: digitizing the novellas along with transcriptions from the interviews we do each year with youth who have migrated. These would be archived in Farendé's cyber alongside another digital initiative: the collection and curation of the writings of Farendé researchers trained by an early French missionary. Their writings from the 1960s and 1970s are vivid, sometimes brilliant, accounts of local culture and ceremony, language and history, and early missionary work—a treasure trove of scholarly writing that today is molding away in suitcases and closets in family homes.[2] These writings are easily digitized with a scanner that costs $300. Another digital initiative the students are working on consists of collecting oral histories from village elders about Kabre origins. These are fascinating, often contested histories with contemporary political implications.

But the local success of this public culture initiative and of the writers' workshop gives pause: these are not projects that return income and only with difficulty are read in instrumental terms. How, then, can one interpret this phenomenon—of precarious farmers embracing the novel, of villagers eager to archive the writings of their forebears? In addition to aesthetic considerations—that youth enjoy the pleasures of writing—I read them as signs of and as aspiration for the modern, tapping into and enlisting local desire in the dream of modernity and global citizenship, thus refusing Farendé's abjection from a world in which today's global has seemingly passed it by (Ferguson 1999; Piot 2010).

Note that these are all low-intensity and mostly inexpensive, sometimes free, interventions that focus largely on human potential and things immaterial—that is, textbook DIY in a neoliberal age. Moreover, they tap into youthful energy on both sides: opening doors of desire for Farendé youth while hitting U.S. students in their soft spot. American students are digital creatures sutured to their devices and, at least in this context, enjoy teaching others how to use them. Student engineers enjoy building things (connecting solar panels to battery packs and laptops, laying and sealing PVC pipe); English majors relish the opportunity to teach writing; global health students will dive into almost anything health-related. This is the upbeat, utopian side of student culture today, an impulse I find hard to resist.

To repeat a point made in the introduction to this volume, and for me an article of faith, accessing local knowledge is key to success. This should be obvious when it comes to interventions that touch on local technique. Introducing a mechanical nut sheller to replace the manual processing of baobab seeds, for instance, requires familiarity not only with techniques of processing (to redirect them toward operating and repairing a mill) but also with local regimes of rights and access. Who owns and cares for the new device? How should gender and age orient access? These are not easy-to-answer questions. While the Kabre do most of their work in groups, they do not own property together. Thus, while fields are collectively cultivated—I work your fields today; you work mine tomorrow—each field and its produce is individually, not communally, owned. Whenever collective ownership has been introduced into the area, it has not worked.

The Kabre will fight and fail to cooperate when there is no clear (single) owner or line of authority. As one man put it, "Who will command whom when it comes to caring for something owned together?" In this case, who will "own" and repair the nut sheller?

Local conventions of labor, ownership, gender, and hierarchy complicate every such event. And—a village verity—the outsider is usually at pains to find resolutions and invariably will commit errors of judgment. It is much better to let villagers sort things out themselves, according to local protocols and organizational principles.

But the same point—the need for vernacular understanding—is also true of nontechnical interventions. Starting a writers' workshop and installing a cyber café depend on knowledge about local literacy. One of the surprising findings of Caitlin Moyles (this volume) was that Farendé students who enjoy reading outside class are made fun of and have to conceal their books. This is certainly a powerful obstacle to getting students to attend a writers' workshop. Or how does one deal with local views that computer use may lead to witch attacks—with users afraid to open messages or attachments from those they do not recognize?[3] This view has clear consequences for computer literacy, and one that a Duke student may need to be aware of before beginning her classes.

Some technical expertise and sociocultural knowledge is indispensable to project implementation. So is knowledge about local politics. Project after development project in this area has foundered because protocols were not followed or authorities were not consulted, or because jealousy interfered. Initiatives like these are forever vulnerable to chiefly overreach—to local authorities who want to be in charge of all that happens in their realm and to profit from them financially. Thus far we have been fortunate to keep Farendé's and Kuwdé's chiefs at bay—another advantage of not only remaining small in scale and flying below the radar, but also of years of building relationships with chiefs (including the occasional greasing of palms). There are also influential civil servants in Lomé who have an abiding interest in the villages and are prepared to run interference if things go awry. Still, the delicacy of the relationship to power is real and gets factored into all that we do.

We had a near-miss with a chief three years ago while organizing a conference with local healers and biomedical professionals (see Rotolo, this volume). The Duke students invited healers they had interviewed throughout the summer, including this chief, who was the head of a local healers' association. When he saw the invitation list, he was dismayed that more of his healers were not included and decided to sabotage the conference. The night before, he sent a messenger to the homesteads of invitees to tell them that the conference had been canceled. Serendipitously, I was fraternizing with a workgroup when the chief's emissary entered the homestead where the group was drinking. The young man whispered in the ears of several people in the courtyard—people who, it slowly dawned on me, all were conference invitees. As soon as the messenger left, I asked about the purpose of his visit, and they spilled the beans (partly because the chief who wanted to derail our event was from Farendé and not well liked in Kuwdé). I immediately called the chief on his cell phone and said I had heard there was a "problem" surrounding the conference the next day (while mentioning neither his emissary nor the content of what had been reported to me). He replied that there must have been a misunderstanding and that he was very much looking forward to the event. The conference went off brilliantly, with the chief a robust participant throughout.

But how can one impress on students the importance of local context and local knowledge to development success? In addition to the independent study they take during the semester before they leave, in which they read about West African and Togolese history and culture and about images and stereotypes of "Africa," and in which they do background research for their projects (researching microfinance broadly, for example, before reading what students from previous years have written about Farendé's microfinance scheme), we meet for lunch twice a week throughout their time in the villages to brainstorm and troubleshoot their projects. During these sessions, we hold language lessons and discuss cultural puzzles, oddities, and misunderstandings that have arisen during the week. Throughout, the message is that understanding local history and culture matter, and can make all the difference in a project's success or failure.

Of course, two months is not enough time to acquire deep local understanding. But it is enough to instill an attitude of respect and humility toward the local (and to convey this to those who will follow) and to learn when to ask others for help. It also makes a difference that there is continuity from one year to the next—of student projects and assistants and community partners who have worked with the group. They carry knowledge about projects forward. And the students write up summaries and best practices—dos and don'ts—of their projects, with suggestions for the next generation of students.

While there is no silver bullet or blueprint for this kind of work,[4] the essays in this volume provide a series of how-to—or, better, how-we-did-it, or, maybe, what-to-avoid—lessons for particular projects. The way Duke students set up the Farendé microfinance drew on local NGOs' wisdom in devising repayment incentives. The writers' collective attended to the advice of schoolteachers in drawing students in and making writing attractive. The modest success of the health insurance scheme resulted from the smart idea of a trio of students to compute the savings of each insured member, then make the rounds of homesteads to show individual savings. The cyber has had a series of setbacks, then slow advances, with some rays of light at the end of the tunnel. Here the lesson has been to aim small and remain patient—and to focus on the managerial (how to run a cyber, whom to put in charge) as much as the technical. And so on.

Finally, reiterating another point made earlier, failure ought to be seen as constitutive. Each of these projects has experienced false starts, missteps, detours, profound setbacks, and flat-out failure. Only fifteen families were signed up for the health insurance system after five years in operation. We installed a cyber café that is used more as a charging station than to access computers or the Internet. Some of our microfinancees have taken the money and run. The list goes on.

But for each setback or failure, lessons have been learned, and there have been some modest successes. The projects have more traction today than they did before. Once you accept that failure is guaranteed, it opens the way to exploring why and how things did not work and how they might work better in the future.

Notes

1. There is, of course, much added value—free and volunteer labor—on both sides, without which these projects would be quite different.
2. One of the researchers became a linguist at L'Institut Nationale de la Recherche Scientifique in Lomé; another was a historian who taught in France; and two others were pastors. All were prolific writers on local culture and history.
3. There are affinities here with the computer "virus," of course, which, common to both idioms, often is sent by others with evil intent.

4. For a smart overview of ethnographic field schools for undergraduates, and of much of the broader literature that goes into the dos and don'ts of this sort of student work, see Hawkins 2014.

References

Ferguson, James. 1999. *Expectations of Modernity: Myths and Meanings of Urban Life on the Zambian Copperbelt.* Berkeley: University of California Press.

Hawkins, John P. 2014. "The Undergraduate Ethnographic Field School as a Research Method." *Current Anthropology* 55, no. 5: 551–89.

Piot, Charles. 2010. *Nostalgia for the Future: West Africa after the Cold War.* Chicago: University of Chicago Press.

Index

178; student projects, overview, 9–14. *See also* Farendé, Togo; Kuwdé, Togo; specific projects

Katchawatou, Patrick, 187, 194–95

Kleinman, Arthur, 49

kokode kotong (disease of the womb), 60–61

kotong susoko (bigness disease), 53–55, 76–77, 80

Kuwdé, Togo, 9, 24, 43–44, 59, 60, 70, 100–101. *See also* Kabre culture; specific projects

Langwick, Stacey, 49

latrine sanitation system, 206

Lévi-Strauss, Claude, 48

literacy, 192–93, 206–7, 208

local knowledge/context, 183, 191–94, 207–9

local medicine. *See* traditional medicine, Kabre

Lock, Margaret, 49

Lomé, Togo, 25, 31, 83. *See also* specific projects

loyalty. *See* relationality in Kabre culture

malaria, 5, 75–76, 80, 87, 90, 100, 106

Médecins sans Frontières, 13, 29

medical anthropology, 22, 47, 48–50. *See also* biomedicine; traditional medicine, Kabre

medical pluralism, 63–64, 68, 78–79, 94–95. *See also* biomedicine; traditional medicine, Kabre

microfinance project, 5, 6, 13, 165–66; calculating transactions, 175–76; client selection, 179–83; operating principles, 176–79, 210; outreach, 170–75; sociological context, 183

migration. *See* youth migration

minimal biopolitics, use of term, 13

missionaries, 2

MJF (Microfinance des Jeunes de Farendé). *See* microfinance project

modernity, 116–18

mortality rates, 64, 100

Moyo, Dambisa, 7

neoliberalism, 6, 205, 207

NGOs. *See* nongovernmental organizations

Nigeria, youth migration to, 8, 113

nongovernmental organizations (NGOs), 5–6, 205; health clinics, 74, 101; on youth migration, 113–14, 133. *See also* specific projects

oral histories, 206–7

palu. See malaria

pharmaceutical black market, 94

reciprocity in Kabre culture, 8–9, 80, 168–69, 171, 183

Redfield, Peter, 13

relationality in Kabre culture, 46, 53, 54, 167–68, 173, 183

reputation in Kabre culture, 169–70, 171, 178, 183

rituals, 8–9, 61, 77, 108, 115–16

sacrifices, 53, 54, 72, 74, 115

Scheper-Hughes, Nancy, 49, 51

sex work, 15n7, 122, 124, 169–70

shadow person. *See warito* (shadow person)

snakebites, 61–62

solar power installations, 12–13, 138, 139, 149

spirits, 52, 53, 55, 73–74, 77, 93, 115. *See also* ancestry and body; diviners

student development, 1–5; attitudes required for, 10, 20–21, 37–38, 188; do-it-yourself (DIY) development, 1, 6–7,

student development (*continued*)
205–7; Kabre projects, 9–15, 205–10;
lessons learned, 33–39; villager openness to, 4–5. *See also* specific projects
study abroad programs, 3–4
sumura kotong (bird disease), 62–63
Swanson, Richard Alan, 51

TCM. *See* traditional Chinese medicine
Togo, 6–9, 100. *See also* Farendé, Togo;
Kabre culture; Kuwdé, Togo; specific
projects
traditional Chinese medicine (TCM), 47
traditional medicine, Kabre, 11, 22–23,
25, 28–29, 88, 92; anatomy of, 71–74;
ancestry in, 55; biomedicine and,
47–49, 67–68, 71, 76–81, 84, 87–89,
94–95, 106–7; body, notion of, 51–53;
collaboration in, 79–81, 95, 107; defined in Togolese law, 87; efficacy of,
45–46, 49–50, 51, 64, 72–73, 91, 92,
95; framing, 45–46; future of, 93–94,
97; gendered remedies, 60–63; health
insurance system and, 106–7; as holistic, 74, 92; literature reviews, 48–50,
68–69; methodologies, 46–48, 69–74,
85–86; overview, 44–45; profession-
alization of, 80; stereotypes of, 84;
symbols in, 48; terminology, 47–48; tisanes, 89; toxicity of plants, 29, 95–96;
in urban setting, 83, 89–93, 96–97. *See
also* diviners; healers; house healers

United Nations Convention on the
Rights of the Child, 131

wagas and youth migration, 120, 122,
124–26, 127, 128, 132
warito (shadow person), 52, 60, 73–74
WHO. *See* World Health Organization
wind medicine. *See hilum kori* (wind
medicine)
witchcraft, 9, 48, 73–74, 76, 79. *See also*
diviners
work, use of term, 45–46, 64–65
World Bank, 6
World Health Organization (WHO), 47,
84
writers' society project. *See* Farendé
Writers' Society

youth culture, 12–13, 166
youth migration, 1, 8, 12–13, 140; to
Benin and Nigeria, 8, 113, 120–29;
as child trafficking, 5, 113–14, 131,
132–33; gender differences, 15n7,
121–24; history of, 114, 118; methodology, 118–19; modernity and, 116–18;
motivations for, 126–29, 166, 190–91;
perceptions of, 113–14, 120, 129–31;
risk and safety, 113, 114, 124–25,
132–33, 173; ritual and, 115–16; sex
work, 15n7, 122, 124, 169–70; *wagas*
and, 120, 122, 124–26, 128, 132; writings on, 206